FLATSHARE, HOUSESHARE

The flat- and housesharer's guide to
congenial co-existence

Edward Barrow

COLUMBUS BOOKS
LONDON

Copyright © 1989 Edward Barrow

First published in Great Britain in 1989 by
Columbus Books Limited
19-23 Ludgate Hill, London EC4M 7PD

British Library Cataloguing in Publication Data
Flatshare, Houseshare: the flat- and house-sharer's
    guide to congenial co-existence
    1. Housing. Sharing. Manuals
    I. Title
    646.7
ISBN 0 86287 438 6

Phototypeset by Falcon Graphic Art Ltd
Wallington, Surrey

Printed and bound by The Guernsey Press, Guernsey, CI

CHAPTER 1

Flatshares and houseshares: myths, drawbacks and benefits

Flat- and housesharing have for a long time been an excellent way to cope with the costs of living in a big city. For property owners, having a lodger makes the best use of expensive space; and for young people starting out on their own, flatsharing is one of the most practical ways of finding somewhere to live. Students faced with finding their own accommodation usually end up in some kind of share, and colleges and universities often have their own houses for this purpose. Flatsharing has its own problems – and advantages – and this book is an attempt to give flatsharers some kind of guide to coping with the difficulties and making the best of the advantages.

Everyone who has spent time in a flatshare has disaster stories to tell, with friendships spoiled for life as annoying habits surface in the close confines of the shared abode. Experienced sharers know how to cope with these irritations; others, less tolerant perhaps, never manage to live harmoniously with other people and instead resolve to move into their own flats as soon as they can afford to do so.

On the plus side, sharing provides a remarkable ready-made social network. It is extremely difficult for a newcomer to a big city to meet new people. Clubs and evening classes offer one method of doing so, and one's colleagues are always good for a pint after work – but the common interests seem to thin out rapidly after that and it is very easy just to talk shop. Sharers, however, mingle not only with their flatmates but with their flatmates' friends and relatives, and will soon be assimilated into a powerful and usually supportive network of friends and acquaintances.

Sharers find a night in bearable; the loner in a studio flat sits gloomily in front of the television on the few nights he or she stays at home alone, otherwise the bright lights lure them out, with a consequent drain on the pocket. Washing and ironing nights offer sharers the chance to swap a joke or the latest gossip and split a bottle of wine from the off-licence. The loner either does without alcohol or faces the ignominy of drinking alone, with echoes of parental admonitions ringing in the background. After a hard day at work and a nightmare journey home on crowded public transport, footweary from the walk back with a briefcase that seems a whole lot heavier than it was in the morning, the loner is faced with a cold, empty flat and that morning's breakfast waiting to be washed up; the sharer might have someone else's breakfast to wash up as well as his own, but his conscience can be eased if it is left – after all, whose turn is it anyway? – and a pot of tea, a gin and tonic, with the other sharers in the house is comforting and relaxing.

Sharing does have its drawbacks. Perhaps the biggest drawback is the Bathroom Queue. Nowadays, most people faced with the daily grime of a big city like to take a bath or a shower every day; if there is only one bath between four or five in a flat the morning queue can fray tempers, to put it mildly. The only practical solution to this problem is to have more showers and baths; most Victorian houses were designed with rather less frequent bathing in mind. For three people, one bathroom is adequate. For four, it may just be, provided the loo is separate. For five, a second bath or shower is no longer a luxury; six and more people sharing one bathroom will smell. It helps if some of the inhabitants can manage with an evening bath and need to use the bathroom only for a wash in the morning. Generally speaking, women seem more able to cope with this arrangement; men like a bath or a shower in the morning because it makes shaving easier.

Shared living is made all the more effective if meals are

regularly shared. Many sharers shy away from organizing communal meals, except perhaps for special celebrations, but once a sound and flexible system has been worked out the advantages of shared meals are huge. Not only is the effort greatly reduced, it being as easy to cook for five as it is for one, but the mess is reduced, and everyone ends up eating better food more regularly.

Sharing has particular benefits for those who are studying for professional examinations. If you are, for example, an articled clerk with a firm of solicitors, or a trainee accountant, you will have a large amount of studying to do in your spare time. A shared flat is an excellent environment in which to do this work, particularly if there are others in the flat with the same problem. Studying becomes less of a bind if there is someone else in your immediate environment doing it, and the knowledge that a proper meal will be prepared for you (unless it's your turn to cook) will reduce the temptation to nip out to the take-away and the off-licence, perhaps calling in at the pictures en route. Your flatmates will be watching over you, to make sure you work; it is much easier to fool yourself that you are working hard than it is to fool them. The same benefits, of course, apply to full-time students in a flatshare. However, the downside in both cases is that you may all become so disaffected with studying that the slightest excuse will see books abandoned at opening time.

There are various myths about flatshares. One of them is the 'marker-pen-on-the-milk-bottle' myth: the idea that sharers end up getting so possessive about their own milk, fruit juice or alcohol that they deliberately mark the bottles to deter 'borrowing'. Perhaps some people do get that neurotic; I have lived in many different shares and I have never come across anything approaching such selfishness, although I do recall a row breaking out when the orange juice I bought to make buck's fizz on Sunday morning disappeared into someone else's Harvey Wallbangers on Saturday night.

Another myth is that shares don't work where couples are involved. I have lived as a couple in a share and as a single with other couples and it has (up to a point) always worked satisfactorily. Very often the failure of a flatshare with a couple has been blamed upon the existence of the couple, but there is usually some other reason why the share failed. Possessive people generally make bad flatmates and couples need to be laid-back enough about their relationship not to become possessive towards each other (this is a topic to which I will return in a later chapter).

A particularly pervasive myth is that single-sex flatshares are better. After going to a single-sex school and a single-sex college at university I always lived in mixed flatshares and I have no doubt that mixed is best. The hothouse atmosphere of a single-sex environment is simply no fun, and while adolescents always find it hard to distinguish between amicable companionship and full sexual relationships, a mixed share is far more civilized and helps both sexes learn about the opposite sex in a reasonable and decent manner. There is no evidence at all that mixed houses are dens of iniquity and promiscuity; indeed, quite the reverse is true. In single-sex houses it becomes important to demonstrate one's virility, or attractiveness, by successfully 'pulling' bedmates, while in mixed houses everything is less competitive and more relaxed, which makes it much easier to lead a satisfying and fulfilled love life. In single-sex houses, the conversation turns around sex; the men in all-male houses tell revolting dirty jokes to each other to calm their frustration and to demonstrate their vast experience of life and women, but in a mixed house the conversation covers a far wider range of topics and although sex takes its due place in the conversation it is to a far smaller degree a matter for braggadocio.

Many flatshares are in rented flats or houses, and the common enemy in this instance becomes the Landlord. Landlords vary from being absurdly possessive about their property – banning posters from the wall, prohibiting cats (and even goldfish), and forbidding the use of onions in cooking. Others are less fussy but have various peculiar foibles. One landlord I had was happy to let his house go to ruin – we complained frequently about leaks, which he never repaired – but spent a lot of time and money repairing the stained glass in the front door after it had been broken by a burglar just before we moved in. Landlords usually let shared houses on licences, which generally give the tenant no security of tenure. In the terms of the licence are hidden a number of outrageous rules forbidding, for example, overnight guests, playing music after 10 o'clock at night or the use of heaters other than those provided. Of course, the landlord turns a blind eye to the rules – until he develops a grudge against his tenants, at which point he has full recourse to the small print in the licence agreement.

There is, however, one feature which all landlords have in common, and that is quite execrable taste in furniture and decor. This is a feature which they share with the previous owners of the house or flat you have just bought; the difference is that with a house or flat of your own you are free to repaint the walls, while in a rented house or flat you are forced to tolerate the ghastly colour schemes, revolting carpet and hideous furniture all the time.

It's important for everyone living in a flatshare to want to make it work. Shares are usually run informally, and the rules are mostly unwritten. The rows develop when people use different sets of rules. This book is not intended to provide a standard set of rules, but I have included a number of hints as to how best to cope with living in a shared house and how to derive the greatest benefit from what can be a highly rewarding way of life. Above all, sharing is about *friends*. Since I started living in shared houses and flats, I have made many very good friends and have met many more people who have in some way or another added to the quality of my life through shared living. I hope that one or two more people may gain in the same way after reading this book.

CHAPTER 2

Types of flatshare

There are many different types of flat- and houseshare; some are rather pleasanter than others. In this chapter I describe seven stereotypical shares; the characters are entirely fictitious, but I hope that they are none the less recognizable.

(1) The student slum

The Young Ones, in the television series, lived in a stereotypical student slum, complete with stereotypical students. The washing-up is seldom done, other cleaning never. The fridge contains rotting vegetables and milk culture in several different stages of growth. Cups or mugs for tea and coffee are given a cursory rinse before use and never washed afterwards; the sugar is kept in the bag complete with lumps from a wet spoon. Only the young and effective immune system of the inmates prevents permanent dysentery, but their bowel movements are seriously irregular thanks to regular intakes of SuperStrong Lager or MacHeady's Old Disgusting Ale and the subsequent macho vindaloos.

The sitting-room carpet is stained and torn, and the house reeks of stale beer, vomit and cigarette ash. Occasionally the finer sensitivities of the inmates prevail and they attempt to cover up the smell by burning joss-sticks. This is not as effective as fresh air would be, but none of the windows have been opened for years.

The bedrooms in such a house smell of sweaty clothes. Students wash as infrequently as possible, mainly because the hot water comes from an ancient geyser which requires several hours' pre-heating before being able to produce a bare trickle of hot water. The bath can best be described as leprous. Laundry collects until the end of term, when it goes home to Mum's multi-programme automatic.

These students are still learning about life and getting on with one another. Being male (women would never tolerate such conditions), they imagine cleaning and tidying does itself, and live in filth until, come the end of term, it does.

Sometimes the student slum is inhabited by non-students, which makes life a bit more difficult as there is no end of term. Sometimes, too, it is a squat – no landlord to check up on things.

(2) The secretaries' sanctuary

The secretaries' sanctuary is altogether more salubrious. Its inmates are usually secretaries, cooks or nurses. They are all female. The washing-up, hoovering and tidying are always done, but perhaps the dusting and the polishing may be forgotten once in a while. Each of the sharers has her own pet hate and a particularly irksome habit which is the pet hate of one of the others. Kate gets so mad when Fiona borrows her *Cosmo* before she's finished with it but Fiona can't see what the fuss is about. Fiona gets mad because Irene always slams the door and leaves her slippers in the sitting room, and Irene can't stand Kate's Meatloaf tapes. Apart from that, they all get on fine. The talk is of men – the dishy one at the office, the groper on the tube, the weirdo who follows them home. They each have their own boyfriends, and quite often spend the weekends away. They seldom go out as a group, apart from the occasional foray to the local pizzeria to marvel at the machismo and unashamed phallism of the waiter with the pepper-mill. Their main social event, however, is the dinner party. They hold one at least once a week, inviting their friends, cousins and relatives in an attempt to make a better match for their flatmates than their present one. They go out to dinner parties too, almost as often. Their food is always immaculately dull, copied, according to culinary skill, from *The Cordon Bleu Cookbook* or one of Marks & Spencer's glossy recipe collections. Each has a special dish which she cooks well and prefers to anything else. Kate makes a brilliant lasagne, which - it must be admitted – is good of its kind. Fiona is the dab hand at chocolate mousse, while Irene makes a wonderful starter with tuna fish.

Men never feel at ease in the secretaries' sanctuary. The tidy bathroom with its feminine ephemera of shower caps and tampons makes them uncomfortable, but the most off-putting thing of all is the rack of tights draining over the bath. But for all their faults, the girls in the secretaries' sanctuary do help each other out. They share their emotional problems and their successes, and are quite happy to conspire together for the benefit of each other, complaining about employers, boyfriends, parents and the rest.

(3) The couple and the lodger
The Couple, Philip and Sarah, are not married. In any case, they've just bought their own flat, and the mortgage repayments are killing them. They do so want to get new curtains/carpets/bathroom, etc. but they just can't afford it. Soon, of course, Philip will get a rise and it won't be so bad but their little dream nest is not quite the same with the previous owner's naff taste still so much in evidence. Luckily they had the good sense to get a two-bedroomed flat – Sarah's parents made that a condition of their putting in the cash that helped them buy it, because then at least they could imagine that the couple slept in separate rooms. But Sarah and Philip might as well let out the room to a lodger, who'll pay his rent weekly in cash. With that little extra, they'll be able to afford to get the extra bits and pieces they need. Roger the Lodger is a new arrival in Philip's office, and he's a very nice boy really. Sarah mothers him a bit, showing him how to do his laundry and occasionally tidying his room. It's OK for him for the time being, but he doesn't really get on with Philip and Sarah, who are just that little

bit older. They're always a bit curious (and, if the truth be known, slightly envious) when he comes back in at three, dropped by a taxi whose rumbling diesel engine wakes them before they hear his footsteps on the landing. But living with them cramps his style a bit, since he can hardly ask his friends back for coffee when he feels like a guest in someone else's home. And that invitation for coffee, after all, is only the preamble to other activities. In fact it all works out quite well, because he moves out just as Philip gets his promotion.

(4) The earnest regiment

Type 4 houses and flatshares live by rules. There are rules for everything, reinforced by rosters. The punishment for disobeying the rules is at least a week's Coventry, and at the second offence it's dismissal. However, everyone in this house is so earnest that the rules are never broken. There's a big kitchen, with a large kitchen table, a dresser, a gas fire and one very tatty easy chair, as well as a porcelain sink with a scrubbed-clean wooden draining board and an Interesting Kitchen Windowsill with two germinating avocado seeds perched on cocktail sticks over jam-jars. The most important feature of the kitchen is the Notice Board, because the house is run by the Notice Board. Perhaps the Notice Board even has a life of its own, greater and more powerful than any of the people who live in the house. Everything in the kitchen is strictly communal, and one of the House Rules – Number 8, Section 6, Subsection 3 – runs as follows: 'No person shall leave anything of theirs in the Kitchen. Anything Left in the Kitchen which belongs to someone will be Burned or Given to the Brownies.' The kitchen is where the communal meals are served, at Seven O'Clock Precisely. Everyone is always in for meals, except at weekends, when no one is in. Breakfast is slightly less formal, but there is an Early Morning Tea Roster and a Breakfast Washing-up Roster as well as a Roster for the Evening Meal Cook and the Evening Meal Washing-up, and a Hoovering Roster and a Roster for Cleaning the Toilets.

9

Finances in this house are by means of a Kitty. The
Kitty is the source of all the arguments, mainly because
Sue – who does most of the shopping – buys oranges, for
everyone's health, but she is the only one who actually
eats them. What really irks Vinny is that Sue keeps on
buying Outspan oranges, despite the motion carried at
the last House Meeting that they would boycott South
African produce. Sue, on the other hand, gets mad at
Jack, who does all his shopping at Marks & Spencer and
spends as much on one meal as Sue does on five. By and
large, however, they all rub along pretty well, but after
the evening meal they all repair to their own rooms –
there is no communal sitting room – which prevents any
arguments about what television programme is watched.

(5) Casa Borgia
Everyone who lives at Casa Borgia is doing all right,
with an ample income. Right now, however, they're too
young to worry about property and becoming settled,
so they have a good time. The house is fluid, varying
from three to ten inhabitants, but in fact there are five
bedrooms. There are two couples who keep the place
together, Alison and Richard and Liz and Mike. They
all met at University, where they were very settled, but
somehow the fizz has gone out of both relationships.
Richard's job means he has to spend quite a lot of time
in the States, and it was on one of those occasions,
when Liz was visiting her parents, that Alison and Mike
ended up in the sack. Of course, it was only the result
of a drunken evening, but all sorts of rows ensued, rows
which had been simmering for a long time. Alison was
quite keen for the event to become common knowledge,
because she wasn't at all keen on being left behind while
Richard was abroad and she had been building up to a row
with Liz anyhow. Liz was pretty mad about it, needless
to say, but in fact she'd bumped into an old flame that
night and gone back to his place, although Mike never
heard that side of the story until years later. Then Penny
moved in to one of the other rooms, and before long she
and Richard were having an affair.

Alison got a job abroad, she moved out and Liz moved in her new man. Mike, meanwhile, had fallen for Mary, one of his colleagues and she started to spend a lot of time at the house without actually moving in – although her room-mate had now got a regular boyfriend, which made life awkward at her Chelsea boxroom. Backstabbing and infidelities went from bad to worse. After a party Richard, Mary and Alison (back for the party) ended up in one bed (they deny to this day that anything happened, because they were all too drunk) while Mary's room-mate was with Mike in another and Penny and Liz's new man were in a third. Mary's room-mate's new man and Liz went off for a dawn walk, seeing that they had lost their partners, and ended up in an hotel room in Brighton; three weeks later they moved in together in a little flat in Tooting Bec. Despite all this, the Casa Borgia crowd remain good friends and the house still gives parties renowned far and wide for their excellence.

(6) The commune
The commune is a timewarp from the early 'seventies. The house belongs to Rosie, who inherited it from her grandmother. Rosie is a painter, who works in the attic, which makes a good studio, and she is moderately successful; for a painter, this means no more than being able to survive without Supplementary Benefit. She is supported by Dave, a journalist on the *New Left Review*, and in the same house live Alex, an American woman who had a bit of a funny time with LSD when she first came to Britain before being rescued and mothered by Rosie; Typhon, Alex's 5 year-old son; Alan, a 40-year-old hippy who works for the council, in the housing department, and sings in a folk club on Wednesday and Friday nights; and Karma and Sutra, two beautiful Persian cats. Karma and Sutra are the only members of the household permitted meat; they were fed on a wonder vegetarian cat food for a fortnight before their wailing and straying made even Alex agree to allowing them Whiskas again. Dave is very dubious about the vegetarian crusade, considering it a self-indulgent bourgeois craze, but he accepts it for

11

the sake of harmony and because Rosie says it's good for
his health to have a meatless diet. When nobody is looking he sneaks out for burgers and kebabs, justifying it to
himself as a means of keeping in touch with the eating
habits of the masses. They've stopped being macrobiot-
ics now, but they still eat only brown rice, brown flour
and brown sugar. Typhon is a precocious and spoiled
brat whom Rosie, Alan and Dave try to discipline from
time to time, but Alex's indulgence always wins. He is
not allowed guns, and an almighty row followed on one
occasion when Alex relented to his whining and bought
him a Darth Vader Death Ray Emitter on the grounds that
it wasn't a gun so much as a toy, and anyway you've got
to let the boy have some fun once in a while.

The house has a garden which is in a terrible mess
despite several house resolutions to grow organic herbs
and vegetables. However, the residents do make their
own yoghurt, in a Taiwanese electric yoghurt-maker.
While they are all agreed about boycotting South Africa,
often go on anti-apartheid marches and are all paid-up
members of CND, they can't agree about Israel. Dave is
pretty solidly anti-Israel – though careful not to be anti-
semitic – because of its regional imperial hegemony and
because it's paid for by the Americans, but Alex comes
from New York-Jewish stock and regards the king of
Saudi Arabia as a terrorist. As a compromise they peel
the Carmel labels off the avocado pears before bringing
them home.

Despite their vegetarianism and concern for healthy,
organic food they all (with the exception of Typhon and
the cats) smoke heavily. But you won't find a cigarette
packet in the house; they all roll their own. They don't
smoke anything else nowadays, although all of them were
once regular smokers of marijuana and in the wild, free
days of the early 'seventies they used to do a bit of acid
as well . . . except Rosie, who was always too sensible
(or cowardly) for that; but even she still speaks with
reverence of the psychedelic age and incorporates its
imagery in some of her more way-out paintings, being
loth to admit that in fact she never gave it a go. They did

once grow their own marijuana, years ago, but now it's no longer quite so socially acceptable among the radical Left in Thatcher's Britain, and none of them really wants the inconvenience of getting caught. Besides, not one of them now has the street credibility to go and buy any, and Alan's job in the housing department has shown him the less pleasant effects of harder drugs. Cocaine has never come their way, being far too bourgeois, so they stick to alcohol – buying their wine by the case from the local wine warehouse. Dave used to make home-brew, but decided the kits contained too many chemicals and now goes to the pub for beer.

Finances are haphazard; no one has paid Rosie any rent for years but all the bills are split amongst the other three, so Rosie lives almost for nothing, which is fortunate because that's roughly what she makes from her paintings.

(7) The male yuppie and the deb
Charles lives in Fulham, where he has bought a flat on a cheap mortgage, courtesy of his City job. He doesn't have time for a social life, apart from a round of drinks parties before Christmas, but feels that he needs a woman in his life. Caroline is his schoolfriend Toby's sister. She was looking for somewhere to live after finishing at the Cordon Bleu school and getting a job as a directors' cook for one of the merchant banks. She's quite pretty in a hooray sort of way, just Charles' type really. Of course, her parents had known Charles before and they were quite happy for her to share a flat with him; after all, the pair weren't romantically involved and it was probably a lot safer in London for a girl to have a man around in case of any problems with weirdos. Charles doesn't need the money, he's got pots of it from his outrageous job, but he likes the company and having someone to wash up his breakfast things. Caroline is quite happy to cook for him from time to time and in return he takes her out for meals at various chi-chi restaurants in Fulham. Besides, she's always got things left over from work which she brings back – the occasional pot of goose pâté, bits of smoked

13

salmon, and so on. But he makes sure she pays her rent – in cash of course, no point in telling the taxman about it, is there? – and her share of the bills. In fact, the only thing missing from this cosy relationship (from Charles' point of view) is the carnal side. He's much too much of a gentleman to make a pass at Caroline, but it flatters his ego to have a pretty girl around. In time, of course, they get on better and better with each other; people start asking them out as a couple and before very long Charles completes the set; Caroline continues to pay rent but they now have a spare bedroom (where Caroline still keeps her clothes for the days when Mummy calls round after a trip to Liberty's or Harvey Nicks).

The best flatshare is like none of these stereotypes, but most flatsharers will recognize elements of their own place in one or two of these descriptions, and see their flatmates in some of the characters in these vignettes.

You won't, I hope, be as untidy as the students in their slum, as interfering in your flatmates' lives as the secretaries in their sanctuary, as incompatible as the couple and their lodger, as bossy and earnest as the regiment, as disloyally promiscuous as the inmates of Casa Borgia, as hypocritically right-on as the communards or as conveniently fashionable as the yuppie couple in Fulham, but you will, surely, support, co-operate and co-exist with each other.

CHAPTER 3

How to find a flatmate

The strongest single determining factor in whether or not a flatshare is a success is the compatibility of those who live there. It's very hard to assess compatibility, but when you are choosing a new flatmate you are more likely to make the right decision if you have a wide choice. For this reason, my advice is always to advertise, even if you have a friend who is looking for a place. If you don't happen to get on with the person you choose from an ad you can always give him or her notice without difficulty. Your friend, on the other hand, may be allergic to cleaning the bath or have some other disgusting habit of which you were blissfully unaware, and it's far harder to tell a friend that you can stand it no longer. The consequences, too, will be much more painful than it would have been to make your excuses *before* embarking upon such enforced intimacy.

Many people, however, prefer to use the grapevine when looking for co-sharers, perhaps because they are nurturing an unreasonable fear of the stranger who might arrive on their doorstep in response to an advertisement. There may also be a fear that advertising will render the whole arrangement more subject to legalities. Since most mortgage agreements prohibit sub-letting and tax is seldom paid on rent, some owners are reluctant to formalize matters at all through an advertisement and would prefer to keep the breaches of the law, and their mortgage agreement, 'in the family'. An additional advantage of using the grapevine is that it is cheaper, but against this has to be weighed the disadvantage that your room may well be unoccupied, and therefore not producing rent, while you wait for the grapevine to come up with a candidate.

ADVERTISING
There is quite a wide range of possible advertising media.

Shop windows Newsagents' windows are certainly cheap and are used by old-fashioned landladies with digs to offer. Their accommodation cards are written in spidery old-fashioned handwriting, offering 'clean rooms' to 'respectable working gentlemen'. Sometimes they advertise large rooms for two girls willing to share, and very occasionally a genuine flatshare or houseshare is advertised. But by and large the market is slightly different to that of the flatshare columns seen in the press. Each window card, space for which costs a few pence for a week, will reach a very limited, local audience. Getting wider coverage will mean a lot of footwork for doubtful extra benefit.

The Student Union notice board This, a close relative of the newsagent's window, has various equivalents in the notice boards of hospitals and other institutions. If you need to find people to fill a college house, or you or your landlord will only allow students or nurses or whatever in the house, the SU notice board is a good place to advertise. Usually you'll be at least faintly acquainted with the people who answer such an advertisement – it's halfway between open advertising and the grapevine.

National newspapers *The Times* and *The Guardian* both have dedicated flatshare columns, but although the papers are national the area covered is almost exclusively London. *The Times* generally gives a wider coverage and many London flat-hunters buy it specifically for the purpose. *The Guardian*, with its slightly more radical politics, usually produces flat-hunters who share some of the same political inclinations as the newspaper. As far as I know, none of the other national newspapers runs a regular flatshare column; I have, however, come across a two-column display advertisement for a houseshare in the *Financial Times*: clearly the advertiser was looking for sharers from within a very specific group of people and was prepared to pay to be selective.

Local evening papers The best bet of all is generally the local evening paper. In London, the *Evening Standard* has a flatshare column every day; other evening papers may concentrate their flatshare classified advertising on certain days of the week. By using a local paper you reach virtually all your target market, given that anyone in your town looking for somewhere to live is likely to buy the paper and scan its flatshare columns. The cost may be fairly high but it is usually well worth while. On occasion I have received over a hundred replies from a single advertisement in the London *Evening Standard*.

Wording your advertisement
The words of your advertisement should be carefully worked out. Your objective is to make the place seem as attractive as possible, in order to get a large number of replies and give yourself the widest choice of future flatmate.

Location The standard form is to begin by stating the part of town where the flat is located. You can be slightly devious here: you can refer to the area either by name or by postcode. You must use your judgement to decide which would be the most appealing.

Type of sharer Are you looking for a man or a woman? You can give some idea of the size of the house or flat, by using an ordinal number: '3rd girl' (i.e. others are two girls already); '4th pers (f)' (there are three people and you're looking for a fourth, who should be a woman); '3rd m' (there are two men already, looking for a third); '4th gay m pref n/s' (fourth gay man for a gay male flatshare, who should ideally be non-smoking); 'f veg n/s' (a non-smoking vegetarian woman).

What you're offering Is it a flat or a house? Mixed- or single-sex? Any special features? Selling points are the closeness of public transport, and in London particularly the Tube, the type of place and the facilities. The type of place can only be summarized briefly – 'lux', 'lovely', 'friendly', etc. are in any case subjective terms, but help to make your ad stand out from the rest. Facilities are summarized in a standard set of abbreviations:

o/r	= own room
c/h or ch	= central heating
ctv or col tv	= colour tv
w/m, wm or wash mach	= washing machine

and so on.

Rent should always be stated, as either inclusive ('incl') or exclusive ('excl' or 'plus bills') of heating and lighting expenses and quoted per week ('pw') or per calendar month ('pcm').

The contact time and number is the other essential. The ad should end with a phone number, and when to ring. This is sometimes abbreviated to 'eves' (or 'evgs') but it's better to be more precise –'aft 6' or 'aft 7' – since people's ideas of what time of day constitutes evening vary.

Don't include a work number in the ad. If you have phrased it openly, you will get a load of replies and you shouldn't expect your employer to tolerate the incoming calls on the office phone. Quite apart from the company time involved in answering them, you and your phone line will be unavailable for business calls. If you have spare holiday to take, it could be a good idea to have an afternoon off, but you could be wasting your half day off if for some reason the advertisement doesn't appear. If you have a reasonably tolerant employer, it might be worth planning to take the afternoon off, buying the early edition of the local paper at lunch time to see whether the ad has appeared, and – provided your employer is an amenable type – going back into work if it hasn't.

The market for rooms in a flatshare is seasonal. Demand

peaks in September and again in January; it is at its slackest in May. Unfortunately, you don't often have the choice; if a room becomes vacant in May you will want to fill it immediately. In September you can expect to have a vast queue of applicants. Don't be put off by this; it is possible to interview scores of people in an evening.

The ads I and my co-sharers placed came to be standardized over time to the following:

> **Clapham Sth:**5th pers to
> sh friendly mixed hse nr
> Tube. O/r, c/h etc. £xxx
> pcm excl. Tel 123 4567.

It's worth going on to four lines rather than two or three so that your advertisement stands apart from the rest, and one or two whole words make the copy more attractive, so that the customer – the flat-hunter – is drawn to your advertisement first.

Fielding the replies

The telephone rings. At the other end of the line a flustered voice says, 'It's about the flat . . .'

Me: 'Yes . . .'
Caller: 'Has it gone yet?'
Me: 'No, it's still available . . .'
Caller: 'Can you tell me a little more about it?'
Me: 'What would you like to know?'
Caller: 'Well – what about the other people there?'
Me: 'There are four at the moment, two men and two women, and we're looking for a fifth. We are all professional people and we're aged from 22 to 30 . . .'
Caller: 'Right. What's the room like?'
Me: 'It's medium-sized, just been decorated. If you got it would you be able to move in at the weekend?'
Caller: 'Yeah – is that all right?'
Me: 'We're seeing people between 7 and 9.30 tonight. Can you come and see it then?'
Caller: 'Oh – can't I come tomorrow? I'm not free tonight.'
Me: 'Well, we'll probably decide tonight. You could try ring-

ing tomorrow, but there's a lot of people coming round tonight
so it'll probably be gone.'
Caller: 'Oh, right. How much is the rent then?'
Me: 'It's in the ad – two hundred a month.'
Caller: 'Oh – yes, so it is. I'll try and come tonight then.'
Me: 'What kind of time will you come?'
Caller: 'Can I come at 6.30?'
Me: 'No – between 7 and 9.30. The others won't be back
by seven.'
Caller: 'Oh – right. Well, I'll be there at 7 then . . .'
Me: 'OK, can you tell me your name?'
Caller: 'Yes – it's John Smith.'
Me: 'OK, John. The address is No XX, Xanthia Road, SW25
and nearest tube is Dog Kennel Road. Have you got an *A-Z*?'

With luck I have managed to pin down the person
to a time and impressed upon him the fact that he will
have to move in sharpish. No point in giving detailed
directions; with an *A-Z* the address is sufficient. This may
sound brusque – and indeed it is; the phone always rings
constantly whenever we place ads and if you have a long,
pass-the-time-of-day chat with every caller you will very
soon be (a) hoarse and (b) fed up with it all.

The interview
There are many different approaches to the interview.
By a process of trial and error we have come up with
a system that works with a large number of candidates.
The numbers you've got to see will shape the way you
run the interviews. We interview on one evening only,
but if we're getting an underwhelming response we might
stretch to two so as to widen the choice. We offer to see
everyone who can come that evening; the only time I
have put people off coming is when we had a list that
was well over a hundred names long. The person you
put off could be the ideal candidate. We do make sure
that people can move in at the right time, however; it's
no use seeing someone who can't move for a month if
you need the room filled at the weekend.

You may well wonder how it is possible to interview
a hundred people in one evening and make a sensible

decision at the end of it all. In fact, it's unlikely that you will actually get a hundred interviewees. Between a half and a third of those who say they are coming won't arrive. But, even so, fifty or sixty people is a lot to see in one evening. No one expects you to remember all the people you see: all you have to do is to try to remember those who appeal to you – those whom, mentally, you shortlist.

The whole household should do the interviewing. It's not always possible to arrange this but those that can't be there have to realize that they will forgo their right of veto on prospective tenants. Since everyone will have to put up with the new lodger, it is very much better if everyone can be at home, and you should all be prepared to cancel minor engagements in order to participate in the interviewing.

Prepare for the session by having the house or flat reasonably tidy, especially the kitchen, sitting room and the room to let. If other people's bedrooms can be tidy, so much the better, as curious interviewees will always want to look in. Have ready a folder with some sheets of paper and a clipboard with the list of names and times. This should be kept in the sitting room. Three distinct rôles will be required during the evening: doorperson, guide and clerk. The Doorperson holds the clipboard, the Guide shows the premises while the Clerk holds the folder. Everyone interviews. From time to time during the evening, you should all swap jobs; the guide has a lot of walking around to do.

As people arrive for the interview, the doorperson will tick off the names on the clipboard and show them into the sitting room. The doorperson and the clerk will talk to them, trying to find out as much as possible. At the appropriate times the guide will lead tours round the house, answering questions and trying to find out information as well. When the guided tour is over, the prospective tenant will be returned to the sitting room, where the clerk will take down telephone numbers and other relevant information, including little notes to help recognition.

By and large it isn't necessary to have a huge list of questions for interviews; inevitably you will start by asking about jobs (or, in the case of students, the statutory 'What are you reading?' line). Be careful not to be too prejudiced for or against, say, accountants or advertising executives, or engineering/computer studies/combined arts/sociology students: there's always an exception to prove the rule under the duffel coat/spectacles/lurid make-up or other uniform. In a college environment, it is a very good idea to share with people who *don't* read the same subject as you: it helps all of you keep a wider perspective on life. You're looking for *compatibility*, above all, which you should be able to sense. The questions and the conversations help, but it doesn't really matter what they or the answers are. Roughly 90 per cent of the people you see you will be able to dismiss out of hand. It seems to me that there is a permanent hardcore of accommodation-seekers, mostly spotty men in polyester suits that don't fit. Unfortunately you can't just tell them to go straight away, but don't waste mental effort trying to remember them. You have to concentrate on making sure that the 'possibles' get the best attention, both from you and from the others. Usually everyone will agree who they are. When the clerk takes the details, he or she should make sure that the 'possibles' have seen the others, and he could try to make 'possibles' stay a bit longer, but usually the hints dropped to the 'no-nos' are picked up by the 'possibles' and they will get the message.

Do try to ascertain that the 'possibles' are actually interested in the place themselves. Often you'll find that people who aren't really interested tell you that they *are* – and then reject you when you phone them with the good news. Try and let 'possibles' know that they are in with a chance.

Immediate no-nos include:

people who come with boyfriend/girlfriend;
people who talk at length about work/study;
people who talk at length about their hobbies;
people whose breath smells of drink or tobacco;

people who make disparaging remarks about other
  interviewees;
people who make overtly political statements;
racists;
people whose conversation includes an irritating buzz-
  word you've never heard of before, like 'staunch'.

People to consider carefully are the emotionally injured, individuals from a different race or class from
the rest of you, people you find physically attractive
(but see below) – and gay men and women, if you are
yourself heterosexual.

The emotionally injured constitute quite a large group
of your potential applicants. A considerable number of
people get thrown on to the housing market as a result of
a messy affair or the breakdown of a live-in relationship. If
you feel that you can cope with your co-sharer's depres-
sion, the inevitable consequence of such a break-up, then
go ahead. But you must have some other positive reason
beyond compassion for wanting this person to move in.
Once he or she is a part of the household, you will have
an obligation to offer support and help and a listening ear;
right now you don't have to make trouble for yourself in
the future. On the other hand, you shouldn't completely
rule out such people; very often you will be their only
hope.

If you are an out-and-out racist or snob, you are
best advised to dismiss out of hand anyone from a different race or class. But if you are like most people you
probably have a subconscious prejudice against people
of a different skin colour or with a different accent
from your own. It is quite possible that the cultural
differences, in diet, religion and the rest, could make
it very difficult for you to share a house with someone
of a different background. But you should, all the same,
be prepared to give extra consideration to those whom
your natural subconscious prejudice initially warns you
against, and make a conscious effort to compensate for
such prejudices. If you, and your co-sharer, adopt a
suitably easy-going approach, you could both find the

experience an enriching one.

People you find physically attractive must be considered very carefully, otherwise you may find that you have ignored their obvious faults. The safest thing is to opt out of the discussions when it gets round to the one you fancy, and let your flatmates decide.

Gay men and women, if you are yourself heterosexual, could present the opposite problem. Owing to the pressure society puts on gay people, most of them end up living in exclusively gay households. In an ideal world gay and heterosexual people would be happy to share houses with each other and respect each other's sexuality, but most gays looking for a share look for their accommodation on a slightly different circuit. On the other hand, if you don't insist on regarding the newcomer solely from the point of view of his or her sexuality, you could find that sharing accommodation with such a person widens your outlook and braks down a few preconceived ideas.

After the interview
The interview will be hard work and by the end of the evening you will be exhausted. If you have been really well organized, you will have a delicious casserole in the oven waiting for this moment; otherwise, phone for a pizza or send a volunteer hero to the chip shop. Alternatively, a glass of wine or a can of beer at the ready for when the last punter exits through the door will do wonders for helping you get down to the business of making a decision.

The first phase is a discussion of the people you have seen, and being able, with relief, to say, 'God, did you talk to that fat one? Wasn't she dreadful?' and such-like. After supper (leave the washing-up until tomorrow) you can be more serious. Go back to the list and try to match the favourable faces you remember with the right name on the list, then make a shortlist. Then discuss the shortlisted candidates against your basic requirements. Will they fit in? What sort of friends do you think they'll have? Are they likely to have lots of heavy-drinking mates who will come back and wreck the place? Will they always be out? and so on. Finally, you will come to a decision. Each of you will have your own favourites, and the winner must be a compromise candidate – preferably no one's favourite but everyone's second choice. It can be a good idea to ring up immediately.

Other methods of finding a co-sharer
Tried, tested and effective as the above method may be, it would be silly for me to pretend that there aren't others. Here are some of them.

The teddy-bear method is a deeply significant psychological test used to determine whether or not the candidate you have chosen is highly-strung, neurotic and self-obsessed or, on the other hand, open, loving, caring and considerate. Naturally, you want to share a house with the latter type, or so the underlying theory behind the method would have it. So at some stage during the interview, one or other of the interviewers throws a teddy-bear at the candidate. If the candidate drops the teddy-bear, he or she is dropped from the shortlist; but the one who hugs the teddy-bear is an automatic choice. (The disadvantage of the teddy-bear method is that it can produce a house full of very laid-back layabouts, who would rather hug each other than do the washing-up.)

Precision interviewing, by contrast, is a technique for the smaller-scale responses. Interviewing is done two or three days after the ad appears. Those replying to the ad are allocated a precise time to attend, and their telephone number is taken. At least fifteen minutes are allocated to each applicant. After all the phone calls have been taken, the evening will need rescheduling: all the applicants must be telephoned and allocated a new time. By this process you achieve two objectives: (1) you weed out the non-serious applicants, and (2) you emphasize how important it is that those who attend are punctual. Before the interview a proper detailed list of questions is prepared. It should be frank and clear, asking personal questions about politics and religion. The answers to the questions do not in themselves serve as a decision-making aid but do help to get people talking. It can be a help to know beforehand if a particular character is violently opposed to homosexuals, for example, particularly if you happen to be gay or to know many gay people; or if they are strict Jews, Roman Catholics or Moslems, all of whom may have religious principles which could affect the life of the flat.

This method has its drawbacks. It is hardly possible to interview more than a dozen candidates in an evening, which is OK if that is the response you have got, but rules the method out for heavyweight responses unless you deliberately limit the numbers to the first however-many who phoned.

Preselection by telephone is another method – sometimes used, however, by single men seeking an adornment to their Fulham *pied-à-terre*. To those on the phone who are male or who don't speak with a suitably hooray accent the reply is always that 'It's gone.' The young girls who reply are interviewed until one passes the attractiveness test, at which point the other interviews are cancelled.

The interview from the interviewee's standpoint
Finding somewhere to live in a large city can be a nightmare. Some people spend ages looking for a flat, while a few manage it quickly. In the last resort, it's the people with the charm and the 'right' face who tend to get the flats most easily. But do not despair – in time, everyone finds somewhere. It's probably better for you to stay on your friend's floor for another week than to move into the wrong place with the wrong sort of flatmates.

Don't expect to get a flat easily or without making an effort. Just as job-hunting needs careful planning, so finding a place to live needs perseverance and thought. The good, well-located or cheap places tend to be heavily subscribed; the grottier places, further out of town, can be easier to get into. Don't expect to be offered the first place you see, and if you come across a place you really like, you shouldn't take a rejection too personally. However, if after a week of seeing many different places you still haven't had any success and you find yourself getting bored with the process, stop, think, and try to work out whether you might be doing something wrong.

What you wear to look at flats or houses may well affect your chances of being accepted, since the current residents will have no time for a full discovery of your hidden depths: you will be judged on first impressions. Although you are not going to be assessed by the same criteria as would apply at a job interview, work clothes, being neutral and probably inoffensive, could well be your best bet, particularly if your casual look verges on the merely scruffy.

Obvious sartorial mistakes can be very off-putting: suits that don't fit, anoraks, acrylic anything, suits worn with trainers, etc. Try to be reasonably tidy – hair brushed, spots under control. Better to be clean and smell of soap than pong of BO and cheap aftershave.

For women, it is important to wear sensible and comfortable clothes. Tarty clothes may wow some men, and if you're young and pretty you won't find it difficult to get in anywhere (sexist but true), but remember that if you're going to a mixed house you'll have to impress the women as well as the men, and women tend to be able to see through the glossy exterior that beguiles men. Go as your natural self, in clothes that you feel comfortable in, and you won't go wrong.

If it helps you feel secure, go with a friend – but preferably another woman or a male friend to whom you are clearly not attached; bringing a boyfriend could indicate that you lack independence.

At the interview, remember that it is a two-way process, no matter how desperate you are. Although the supply and demand of rooms is seldom equal and the odds are stacked against you, there is no benefit to be gained from staying in a place you don't like with people you don't like. You have to find out about the place and about the people, and no one will be offended if you ask questions. Look around; look into the other bedrooms (having asked first); look closely at the bathroom. If you live there, you'll have to use that bath: could you cope with the scum? A very good idea is to glance in the fridge: fridges speak volumes. What type of food is there? Convenience food and sausages, or leftovers from a real meal? Is it your type of food? Is the fridge clean or not as clean as it might be? Is it jammed full of tonic and beercans?

But in the end it will be the existing residents who make the choice. If you want to live with them, you have to make them choose you. Your aim is to be noticed and liked. If you are aggressive and pushy you will succeed in being noticed, but no one will like you. Charm, as always, is the great divider – but really slimy charm is just as offputting as complete charmlessness. If you are accepted, you will be living as an equal with those now placed in judgement over you and they will be regarding you as an equal. Try to relax, don't be shy, and remember that if you don't get this flat there are plenty of others. Smile at your hosts, answer their questions, and don't be afraid to ask your own. Don't just ask what the rent is – it will probably have been in the ad – or other boring details about the let. Ask what the current incumbents do for a living, and how long they've been there ... Try to carry on a conversation. If you've got a particular hobby or interest, bear in mind that others may not find it equally fascinating. Do let them know about it, though, and if they show genuine interest tell them more: you may find you have a lot of common ground.

Finally, don't outstay your welcome. Once you've been done, up and away. Even if you're liked, outstaying your welcome will move you right off the shortlist. Go home, think about the place, decide whether or not you really want it, then forget about it. If you're lucky, the phone will ring to summon you, but if it doesn't, just keep on looking for the next place.

CHAPTER 4

Administration

Successful administration is essential to the success of a share. Bills are a cause of major rows, particularly telephone bills, so it helps to have a system worked out in advance. The other major cause of disruption is traditionally the drinks cupboard, so don't forget to include that in your system of administration.

RENT OR MORTGAGE REPAYMENTS

Accommodation costs money, usually in the form of rent or, if the sharers have a joint mortgage, mortgage contributions. The latter should be paid to a joint bank account, from which the payments on the joint mortgage can be made. The same joint bank account can handle the rates payments, which the monthly amount paid in should include. By far the simplest method of keeping this under control is for everyone to make a regular standing order payment into the joint account.

If there is a non-resident landlord, you will probably all be *licensees*, and you will each be responsible for paying your rent to him. If he agrees to payment by standing order, you will be saved a great deal of difficulty. If, on the other hand, you are *sub-tenants* and pay rent to a *resident head tenant* (because the Rent Acts provide a high degree of security, this is quite rare), you should ask the resident head tenant to take your payments by standing order: it makes life much easier if you don't have to find a working cash machine for two days in a row at the end of each month.

If either a resident or a non-resident landlord wants rent to be paid in cash, you should insist on a receipt for the rent. If you pay rent weekly, you should be provided with a **rent book** in which to record the payments. Keep your receipts, in case of later dispute. Receipts for rent also enable you to claim Housing Benefit if you are unemployed or on a low income. Some landlords are wary of giving receipts for cash rent because they are not declaring the rental income to the taxman. Tenants usually have no security of tenure, therefore you may not wish to press the point.

WHAT RENT TO CHARGE

If you own the house, or are a resident head tenant, you will want to charge a rent to your lodgers that is reasonable and fair to both sides. 'Fair Rent' has a special meaning under the Housing Act 1977 and is explained in Chapter 5; here, therefore, the term 'reasonable rent' will be used. A reasonable rent is one which is agreeable both to the landlord and to the lodger. When you advertise your room, it is a good idea to see what the going rate is for rooms in your area by looking at the advertisements in the paper. Decide on whether you'll go for the top end of the range or somewhere lower down, and fix a rent for the room. If your lodger is prepared to move in at the rent you have fixed, it cannot be that unreasonable. However, increasing the rent for lodgers who are already in residence is another matter. You should hold the rent at the same rate for at least a year, and when you do discuss increases in the rent you should only expect to get an increase of approximately the rate of inflation over the preceding twelve months. Do not expect your lodgers to agree to paying the market rent at rent review time, particularly if the market rents have increased much more rapidly than inflation. You may decide not to increase the rent at all. House shares do not usually last for ever, and sooner or later your lodger will move out; you will be able to charge a high market rent to his or her replacement.

DEPOSITS
Deposits are often taken at the start of a tenancy. The usual amount of deposit taken is a month's rent in advance. This is one sum of money for which receipts should be given and taken, come what may. The purpose of a deposit is to cover the costs of putting right any damage, paying arrears of rent and keeping bills up to date. Deposits are repaid when you move out, less any bills or other amounts owed. Usually these deposits are not interest-bearing.

RATES
Rates are usually included in any rent and paid by the landlord. Occasionally a non-resident landlord will make rates the responsibility of the head tenant, who will then collect them himself. In this case, it makes sense if the rent payable by the sub-tenants is adjusted to include a figure for general rates. However, rates are in the process of being abolished and the new community charge, or 'poll tax', which will replace them is payable by the individual.

WATER RATES
Water rates are paid to the water authority on the basis of the rateable value of the property. As the rateable value lists are so out of date, this method of payment seems a bit daft. Water rates will eventually be replaced by metered charges so that you pay for the water you actually use, but in the meantime there's the Community Water Charge, a poll tax payable to the water authority by individuals. It makes sense for such items to be included in the rent, where possible, since the landlord will probably be responsible for collecting the charge. The exact details of the new system are as yet unknown.

HEAT AND LIGHT
If the heating bills are included in the rent, there is no incentive for tenants to be economical with fuel. For this reason alone I prefer bills to be divided equally,

and rents to be exclusive. An alternative to paying an exclusive rent and periodically shocking everyone with lumpen demands for payment of huge bills is to include an amount in the rent which goes towards the bills, on the understanding that if the bills come to more than this amount there will be more to pay, but if they are less everyone will get a little refund. The best arrangement with both electric and gas bills is to divide them evenly: later in this chapter I suggest ways of doing this fairly with bills covering different periods. However, if there is someone who (for whatever reason) obviously uses more power than everyone else – for example, someone who works from home during the winter, incurring extra heating costs – then an alternative arrangement can be worked out.

TELEPHONE
Ah, yes, this one. No, it cannot simply be divided. If someone rings Australia, the bill is doubled. Even local calls can mount up if a long chat ensues. One system we had, which barely worked, was that we would keep a book and write down all long-distance calls made. The local calls were just shared evenly. Some flats attempt to have a cash-box by the phone for money for calls. I have never known this to work. The cash-box is inevitably raided for cigarette or chocolate money, or to pay the pizza man. Besides, people seldom have the right change, or they persistently underpay on daytime calls. Another system, which seems unbearably bossy but which actually works quite well, relies on the use of a lot of different-coloured and -shaped counters.

For the counter system you need counters of a specific colour for each person. The different sizes of counter represent different monetary amounts, and there is a stop-watch by the telephone, together with a tariff and a piggy-bank. The counters are also kept by the phone. Each time you call you start the stop-watch, and at the end of the call the cost of the call is read from the tariff and counters, of your colour, go in the piggy-bank.

The system usually means the amount paid for calls is

right, over a telephone charging period, to within £1 or so. Its inventor claims that in her flats it always brought things out right to within a penny, but having seen the method she used to calculate it and her very haphazard treatment of the VAT I can only conclude that this was due more to luck than anything else.

The disadvantages of the counter system are that it's wide open to abuse, and depends upon trust between flatmates to work well.

The best system of all involves using a machine called a call logger. These cost quite a lot of money – over £100 – and need to be connected to BT Meter Pulses.

The call logger works from the pulses used by the phone company to work the meter at the exchange which records your calls. As well as buying the logger, you need to arrange for the pulses to be sent down your line. There is a small fee for this of about £1 a month and an initial charge of about £20. The logger prints the details of every call on a roll of paper: number dialled, date, time, duration in minutes and seconds, and cost of the call in pence. You have to program the logger with the cost of a unit.

Now for the clever bit: how do you tell who dialled what number? One house I know used to keep the logger by the main telephone and everybody initialled their call as it printed out. There is, however, a cleverer way. The exchange ignores any number dialled after the last number needed to get through, but the logger does not. So everyone has their own number, an extra figure which they dial at the end of the number they are calling.

The call logger system is much less open to dispute than others. The tapes exist as proof of the call, so calls to Australia are easily identified. However, the mega-bind is wading through the tapes to allocate 6p here, 6p there, to work out the bills.

If you have a telephone from Mercury, you receive itemized bills which list all the calls made. The new BT exchanges also have this facility, but it is not yet available to Joe Punter. However, even itemized bills won't show who made which call.

The perfect system does not exist. However, if any clever electronics buffs are reading this then they may be able to devise it for me, because all the constituent technology is available. It would consist simply of a little black box situated near the place where the telephone wires come in through the wall. All calls would go through this clever box, which would contain a magnetic tape or a floppy disc.

When anybody needed to make a call, they would first dial their own code number, to gain access to the exchange. Personal codes could be secret, if necessary. The little black box would also know if someone is allowed to dial certain numbers – useful if you had a cleaner, say, whom you might want to ring you at the office but would rather didn't use your phone to ring Australia. The little black box would note the number and the details of the call and record it on tape or disc.

Come the Day of Judgement, the tape or disc would be replayed through a computer, so that everybody's calls were listed, together with the cost and the total.

KEEPING THE ACCOUNTS
Almost inevitably someone has to keep the accounts. Ideally, all the bills should be divided immediately and collected from the members of the household. In practice this doesn't work very well because a lot of the charges just don't get paid quickly enough. A central accounting system is highly recommended. The most sophisticated is the double entry system, which, if you are not already familiar with it, will require some application. However, it is logical, precise and, in my opinion, worth the mental effort of getting to grips with it, so I shall endeavour to explain how it works in the pages that follow.

If you wish, you could handle your domestic accounts by means of a home computer. If you already have one, it's worth buying a simple accounting package to help the accounting process, but don't bother buying a computer just for the household accounts. Incidentally, as every accounting package is different, it is not possible to provide standard instructions here.

Before computerizing your accounts it is as well to be clear about how you would handle them manually. The fundamental principle of manual accounts, the double entry principle, is also adopted in computerized systems. Every entry in a book of account has a twin effect and should be written down twice. At the simplest level, let us say that you buy, for £5 cash, a bag of potatoes. The first, and most obvious, part of the double entry is that you have spent £5 and your cash balance has gone down by £5. But you also now have an asset – £5 worth of potatoes in the cupboard. The full double entry is Credit Cash, £5; Debit Potatoes, £5 (a credit is a *negative* entry: you have £5 less cash).

The headings 'Cash' and 'Potatoes' are called 'accounts'. In a house accounting system you are unlikely to want to keep track of your potato consumption: but you will want to know what food you have purchased, so you will have an account labelled 'food': buying the bag of potatoes is then recorded as Credit Cash, £5; Debit Food, £5. Every double entry must have a credit entry and a debit entry, because the essence of every transaction is to take value from one place and add it to another. Double entry bookkeeping is an important principle; if you don't understand double entry, you'll find it much harder to run a fair accounting system. Let's look at double entry in more detail, examining how you would deal with a heating bill.

You probably do not pay your bills immediately, on receipt. None the less, they should be recorded in the accounts, because you have a liability to pay. (Strictly speaking, you have a liability to pay as soon as you use the gas or electricity: but let us say the liability is incurred when the bill arrives.) Suppose you receive a gas bill for £100. When it arrives, you owe the gas company £100, and you have used heating to the value of £100. One of the accounts you keep could be called 'Gas Company', another 'Heating'. If you were to send the gas company a statement (heaven forbid) it would show that you owed them money. If your bank owes you money, it sends you a statement showing a credit balance: so should the gas company's account show a credit balance. The double entry is Credit Gas Company, £100; Debit Heating, £100. A month later, on receiving the rude red bill, you decide to pay the gas company: the double entry for that transaction is Credit Bank, £100, Debit Gas Company £100. The gas company's account now has a debit and a credit entry for £100, and you owe them nothing. But the bank account has a credit entry for £100, while you know that the bank will debit your account by £100. The answer to this apparent contradiction lies in the nature of the bank statement. Your bank statement is not a copy of *your* account with the bank but a copy of the *bank's* account with you. If you are in the black at the bank, as far as the bank is concerned it owes you money and your account is a liability. But as far as *you* are concerned, the bank owes you money and your account is an asset for you. Your records of the bank's account with you will be a mirror image of the bank's records of your account with them. In your books, cheques you write are credits, and debits in the bank's books, while money you pay in is a debit to you and a credit to the bank.

Confused? Don't worry. Double entry bookkeeping always seems confusing at first but it follows a set of rules which work very well as a means of allocating communal costs. (It was developed by medieval monks who lived in a communal society – the first society in which wealth became associated with an institution rather than an individual.)

Back to the gas bill. In practice, at home you don't make two double entries for the gas bill, but one – when you pay it. Credit bank; debit heating. The intermediate stage, a record of the gas company's account, is superfluous if all you are concerned about is the cash.

Now consider another problem. The electricity used is read from the meter every three months. A month before the next reading is due, two months after the last, you have a change of lodger. The new lodger (let's call him B) will have used a month's electricity, while the parting lodger (A) will have used two months'. So just splitting the bill evenly isn't strictly fair. To be accurate, you should take a meter reading when the person moves out. Let's follow this through as a worked example, in detail.

First, let's summarize the data:

Last bill showed: standing charge   £8.00
       meter reading: 7387
       unit price: 5.4p
Reading when Lodger A left: 8212

Let's say there are five people sharing the house.

The standing charge, of £8.00, is allocated strictly by time – it's the same no matter how much electricity is used. In this case Lodger A, who left after two months, will have used one-fifth of two-thirds of £8.

$1/_5 \times 2/_3 \times £8 = £1.07$ (to the nearest penny).

For Lodger B, the standing charge is:

$1/_5 \times 1/_3 \times £8 = £0.53$.

Until the time when Lodger A left, 825 units (8212 – 7387) had been used since the last bill. On the basis that the electricity is shared evenly amongst five, Lodger A had used 165 units (⅕ x 825), as had the other four residents, at 5.4p each, which works out as £8.91 each for the electricity used to that date.

So the following entries should appear in the accounts:

Debit A, £9.98 standing charge
Credit electricity, £9.98

Debit C, D, E & F (the other lodgers), £8.91 each
Credit electricity, £8.91 each time.

When A leaves, the debit balance on his account is the amount he owes, and he clears the account by paying cash.

This goes,   Credit A,   £9.98
  Debit cash,   £9.98

A month after B arrives, the electricity bill comes, showing that an additional 450 units have been used, i.e. 90 units each, which at 5.4p is £4.86 per person.

The correct entry for the units is therefore:

Debit B, C, D, E, F,   £4.86 each
Credit electricity,   £4.86 each
Debit C, D, E, F,   £1.60 each ($^1/_5$ each of standing
                           charge)
Credit electricity,   £1.60 each

So much for the principle. (I have often thought that it would be much more worth while if double entry bookkeeping were taught at schools rather than such things as quadratic equations; in life we all have to deal with debits and credits – often without really understanding them – and yet when was the last time you needed to solve a quadratic equation? Roughly the same time you did Maths O-level?)

The most useful tool for keeping the house accounts is an analysis book. Bound analysis books are available from commercial stationers such as Ryman's, as are looseleaf sheets. Alternatively you can mark up the pages of an exercise book with a ruler. You need a column for each account – let us say, one for each person in the house and one for gas, one for electricity, one for rates, etc. If you find you've got too many accounts you can combine all the evenly shared accounts into one – 'House Expenses' – but you will lose a bit of detail. Each entry takes one line on the page. Since, under the double entry system, there must be a debit and a credit part to every transaction, you can put both of these on the same line. Credit entries are written in brackets. On each line, therefore, there must always be one entry with brackets and one without. And they must be the same amount. Each line must total across to nothing, because when totalling you *add* the *debits* and *subtract* the *credits*.

Example

You have an electricity bill for £85.50. Let's say you (A) pay it, or agree to pay it. The entry goes: Credit A, debit Heat & Light (see Diagram 1). You write down in the detail line the nature of the bill, then put the amount in brackets in your column and the amount without brackets under 'Heat & Light'. A week or two later a gas bill for £120.25 comes and instead of being paid by you it is paid by B. So the entry in the accounts is Credit B, debit Heat & Light – and the second line of the account is entered as in Diagram 1.

Diagram 1

Details	A	B	C	D	E	Heat & Light
Electric Bill	(85.10)					85.50
Gas Bill		(120.25)				120.25

If you now total the accounts by totalling downwards, you will see that the balances are:

A CREDIT £85.50
B CREDIT £120.25
Heat & Light   DEBIT £205.75

As you are concerned with charging out the heating cost amongst yourselves, you want to reach a position where the Heat & Light Account is zero. You have to make credit entries on the heat and light account of £205.75. But you also know that heat and light is shared equally; £205.75 divided between five is £41.15 each. The next entry is to charge your share to your account: Debit A £41.15, Credit Heat & Light £41.15. If you now do the same for B, C, D and E you will end up with the position as shown in Diagram 2, overleaf.

Diagram 2

Details	A	B	C	D	E	Heat & Light
Electric Bill	(85.50)					85.50
Gas Bill		(120.25)				120.25
Heat & Light	41.15					(41.15)
Heat & Light		41.15				(41.15)
Heat & Light			41.15			(41.15)
Heat & Light				41.15		(41.15)
Heat & Light					41.15	(41.15)

There is a shorter way of doing this entry, as follows:

Debit A, B, C, D, E £41.15 each; credit Heat & Light £205.75 (see Diagram 3).

Diagram 3

Details	A	B	C	D	E	Heat & Light
Electric Bill	(85.50)					85.50
Gas Bill		(120.25)				120.25
Heat & Light	41.15	41.15	41.15	41.15	41.15	(205.75)

The first way is better, because you can see that each line has one debit and one credit entry on it; but the second way is still correct because the line totals to zero across.

Now total the accounts downwards again:

A – CREDIT: £44.35
B – CREDIT: £79.10
C – DEBIT: £41.15
D – DEBIT: £41.15
E – DEBIT: £41.15

This summarizes who is owed and who owes money for the two bills. To settle it up, D could pay B, C could pay A and E could pay £3.20 to A and the rest to B; but it is perhaps easier for A to collect all the money – £123.45

in total – from C, D and E and then pay B the balance he's owed of £79.10, leaving £44.35.

Let's see how each of these options looks when it's entered on the sheet:

Diagram 4

Details	A	B	C	D	E	Heat & Light
Electric Bill	(85.50)					85.50
Gas Bill		(120.25)				120.25
Heat & Light	41.15	41.15	41.15	41.15	41.15	(205.75)
D Pays B		41.15		(41.15)		
C Pays A	41.15		(41.15)			
E Pays B		37.95			(37.95)	
E pays A	3.20				(3.20)	

Diagram 5

Details	A	B	C	D	E	Heat & Light
Electric Bill	(85.50)					85.50
Gas Bill		(120.25)				120.25
Heat & Light	41.15					(41.15)
Heat & Light		41.15				(41.15)
Heat & Light			41.15			(41.15)
Heat & Light				41.15		(41.15)
A Pays B	(79.10)					79.10
C Pays A	41.15		(41.15)			
D Pays A	41.15			(41.15)		
E Pays A	41.15				(41.15)	

For paying *only* the gas and electric bills, this system is a bit of a bind. But where it really comes into its own is for all those other bits of communal expenditure, like the £2.00 paid to the window cleaner by C because he was the only one with any change, or the money for a bag of coal for a fire that cold Saturday afternoon, or the urgent roll of loo paper from the corner shop because someone forgot to put it on the last major shopping list. These can be controlled by using dockets. We use petty cash vouchers, which are kept in a box in the back room: every time someone spends some money, he or she writes it down on a docket. From time to time, when I do the accounts, I empty the dockets from the box and enter them into the ledger. (I do use a computer, in fact, for convenience, but we used exactly the same system before I got the computer.)

Once the dockets have been entered, I staple them together into a bundle and put them in another box which I keep. In an accounts office, the person entering the dockets would probably have to stamp them and initial them. Obviously you don't have to be so meticulous in a house, and there's no reason why you shouldn't throw the old dockets away once they have served their purpose.

Accounting for meals and food
For the purposes of this section, I am assuming that you will be eating communally. In Chapter 7 I describe our meals system, which is reasonably successful. Right now I'm concerned with keeping accounts of expenditure on food.

We work on the principle that the total amount of food eaten by anyone is roughly proportional to the number of evening meals eaten. This isn't always true; for example, you might have someone who goes out a lot at night but eats seven shredded wheats every breakfast-time. If this is the case you'll need to modify the system slightly – for example, counting two breakfasts as equivalent to an evening meal. No system can ever be absolutely fair to everybody all the time, but so long as it's generally fair to most people most of the time you're doing OK.

All the meals dockets are entered in the book, as in Diagram 6. Come the day of reckoning, we add up the total in the food account – in Diagram 6 it comes to £28.50 – and then count the number of evening meals everyone has had since the last day of reckoning, using

Diagram 6

Details	A	B	C	D	E	Heat & Light	Food
Market	(3.50)						3.50
Sainsbury's		(15.30)					15.30
Corner Shop	(1.20)						1.20
Corner Shop			(2.25)				2.25
Supper Items				(3.45)			3.45
Market	(2.80)						2.80

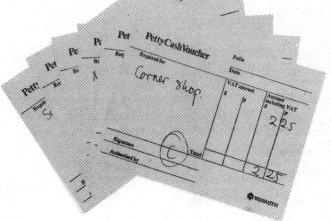

Diagram 7

Cooking/Eating Roster for.......................19.......

NAME:	W	T	F	S	**S**	**M**	**T**	**W**	**T**	**F**	**S**	**S**	**M**	T	W	T	1-16
	1	2	3	4	**5**	**6**	**7**	**8**	**9**	**10**	**11**	**12**	**13**	14	15	16	Total
A					O	I	I	O	I	I	I	O	O				5
B					I	O	I	O	L	I	O	O	I				5
C					I	I	O	O	O	O	O	O	O				2
D					O	O	O	O	I	O	I	O	I				3
E																	0
COOK					C	A	B		D	A	D		B				

the signing-in form – a portion of which is shown in Diagram 7. In this case, A and B have been in 5 times, C twice, D three times and E has been away. So there have been altogether 15 evening meals eaten, at an average cost of £28.50÷15=£1.90 each. This means that A and B each owe £8.50; C owes £3.80 and D £5.70 while E owes nothing. The entries on the accounts to reflect this look like Diagram 8.

Diagram 8

Details	A	B	C	D	E	Heat & Light	Food
Market	(3.50)						3.50
Sainsbury's		(15.30)					15.30
Corner Shop	(1.20)						1.20
Corner Shop			(2.25)				2.25
Supper Items				(3.45)			3.45
Market	2.80						(2.80)
Meals		9.50					(9.50)
Meals			3.80				(3.80)
Meals				5.70			(5.70)

USING A HOUSE BANK ACCOUNT

It is a good idea to have a special account set aside for the house banking facilities. Cheques are written on this account for all the bills, and people pay their dues into it. The accounting treatment is simple – a separate column is allocated to it and it's treated just like any other account. Diagram 9 shows how the previous examples look assuming that the cheques for gas and electricity were written on the house account, while the food was bought by different people. Settlement includes the food, and is paid to the house account. Rent can also be handled by this house account, but although strictly speaking rent should be shown on the ledgers, if it is paid automatically as it becomes due it will get in the way. A single rent account can be used to enable the house bank account to be reconciled with the ledgers.

Diagram 9

Details	House Account	A	B	C	D	E	Heat & Light	Food
Electric Bill	(85.50)						85.50	
Gas Bill	(120.25)						120.25	
Market		(3.50)						3.50
Sainsbury's		(15.30)					15.30	
Corner Shop		(1.20)						1.20
Corner Shop				(2.25)				2.25
Supper Items					(3.45)			3.45
Market		(2.80)						2.80
Meals		9.50						(9.50)
Meals			9.50					(9.50)
Meals				3.80				(3.80)
Meals					5.70			(5.70)
Heat & Light		41.15						(41.15)
Heat & Light			41.15					(41.51)
Heat & Light				41.15				(41.15)
Heat & Light					41.15			(41.15)
Heat & Light						41.15		(41.15)
A Pays	43.15	(43.15)						
B Pays	35.35		(35.35)					
C Pays	42.70			(42.70)				
D Pays	43.40				(43.40)			
E Pays	41.15					(41.15)		

CHAPTER 5

Legal matters

It is an unfortunate fact that the law[1] is not structured to recognize flat- or housesharing. There are many legal pitfalls, and it is potentially a lawyer's paradise. That said, the basis of housesharing is personal relationships, and if they are right everything else follows.

THE HOUSESHARING AGREEMENT
Whether written or not, there is an agreement between every occupier of the house and the owner.

Equal-status tenants and non-resident landlord
In this case, everyone in the house has equal status and pays rent individually to a non-resident landlord. If the landlord has done his homework, there will not be a tenancy or a lease but a licence. There should be a written agreement and it will not usually mention the words landlord, tenant, tenancy or lease. Instead, reference will be made to licensor (landlord), licensee (tenant), agreement (tenancy) and licence agreement (lease). However, despite the carefully worded document, it will still be a tenancy if it can be shown that there is exclusive possession. For this reason the agreement should make it clear that there is no right to use any particular portion of the premises, but a general right to use the whole of the premises in conjunction with other people who have the same right. The landlord will make it clear, at the time that you move in, that he is not letting a particular room to you, but that he is granting you the right to live in the

1 *See* Appendix: Housing Act 1988, p.136.

house with other people who each have the same right.

If you are a licensee, you have no security of tenure and the landlord can ask you to leave at any time in accordance with the terms of your agreement. If he throws you out on the street without notice you should check that this is not in breach of the terms of the agreement. You may be entitled to some limited redress for breach of contract. However, you are not entitled to claim protection under the Rent Acts.

Non-resident landlord and resident head tenant
In this case there is much more security. The resident head tenant has exclusive possession of the whole house, and sub-lets it or licenses it to the sharers. However, the sharers have no security in relation to the resident head tenant, who can evict them in accordance with the terms of any agreement between them. If there is no written agreement the courts will normally assume that four weeks' notice to quit should be given. A written agreement is much better. The nature of the agreement is not relevant in this case as the sub-tenants have a resident immediate landlord and there is no security of tenure under the Rent Acts. The resident head tenant must ensure that there is no clause in the tenancy agreement prohibiting sub-letting, nor should there be a presumption against it. Otherwise, all the sharers have the full resources of the Rent Act at their disposal. At the time of writing, these are considerable, but may change with the introduction of new housing legislation.

If the landlord requires possession, he must obtain a court order. Very often landlords try to gain possession without a court order, by issuing a notice to quit. To be valid, a notice to quit must be in a precisely defined form of words, and even so is merely a prelude to getting a court order. Do not be afraid to take legal advice if your landlord threatens you with eviction. If he is a non-resident landlord, you probably have a good chance of being protected. The best place to go for advice is a local Law Centre, where you can find out what your rights are; the advisor may also recommend you to use a solicitor, who will help you apply for legal aid if you are entitled to it. If the landlord goes ahead with court action, the first you may hear is a summons from the court to attend on a given date. The court will send you details of the landlord's claim and you should consult your lawyers at this stage. They will advise you whether or not to defend the case. If they say no, then find somewhere to live fast. You will have until the date of the hearing, perhaps up to two weeks more. If, on the other hand, they decide that you have a good enough case to make defending it worthwhile, they will advise you how to return the summons form to the court. You then apply for legal aid, through your solicitors, and get on with the defence.

Your solicitors may or may not decide to ask a barrister to represent you in court; although solicitors are allowed to be heard in the County Court, a barrister specializes in court procedure and will have had more experience in cross-examination of witnesses. It is most likely that your solicitors will ask the court for directions at the date of the first hearing. The judge or registrar will give lawyers for both sides a time-table of events leading up to the full hearing, which could be put back several weeks. In the meantime interlocutory proceedings take place, when lawyers obtain the details of the other side's case so that they can prepare their representation. Once all the details have been assembled, the full case will be heard and the judge will decide whether or not he should grant the landlord possession in accordance with the law as it stands. If the landlord is successful, you will have to leave soon – the judge will give a date, but it won't be more than four weeks after the trial date. If no mention was made in the proceedings about the sub-tenants, it may be possible for them to stay on for a while. The landlord may have to get individual court orders against each of them; this will take time, but he will almost certainly be successful.

Resident landlord
If one of the sharers is the freeholder, he or she is

a resident landlord. The other sharers are tenants or licensees, but are not protected under the Rent Acts. Written agreements are seldom made for such arrangements, although a written agreement can help avoid difficulties and misunderstandings. The written agreement is particularly useful if it ever becomes necessary to give notice, as the terms of any notice will be set out in the agreement.

Fair rents
If you have security of tenure under the Rent Acts, which basically means that one of the sharers has a tenancy from a non-resident landlord, the tenant can apply for a Fair Rent. A Fair Rent is determined by the local authority Rent Officer, who will inform the landlord. The Rent Officer will usually visit the property, to measure it and inspect its condition; he or she may also agree to a consultation, which is an informal meeting between the two parties. A Fair Rent is usually lower than the market rent (but there is no guarantee of this) because the Rent Officer is not allowed to take into account any scarcity of rented property. Fair Rents are fixed for two years and apply to the property, not the tenants. If a Fair Rent is fixed, you cannot make a profit from your sub-tenants, although you may charge them more if you provide additional services. The additional services you provide should be worth any extra amount added to the rent; they may not be a sham. Landlords do not generally care for Fair Rents, so while you may be eligible to get a registered Fair Rent if you don't have security of tenure, it is not always a good idea. More information about Fair Rents can be obtained from your Rent Officer – the number is in the phone book.

Restricted contracts
Most house- and flatshares exist under a form of agreement called a restricted contract. Whether there is a tenancy or a licence, a restricted contract will exist if (a) the tenant or licensee shares some of the accommodation with others and (b) he or she has exclusive possession of part of the accommodation – which will usually be a bedroom – and

either (c) the landlord provides furniture and services but not meals or (d) the landlord is resident but does not provide meals. A restricted contract is a curious animal half-way between a tenancy and a licence, and the main feature of it is that there is some form of rent control. There is, however, no security of tenure in the case of contracts begun since 1980, which rather undermines the position of the tenant or licensee seeking a 'reasonable rent'. Reasonable rents are determined by reference to the local Rent Tribunal (not the Rent Officer) and the case may be referred by the landlord, the tenant or the Local Authority. A reasonable rent so determined is not a Fair Rent determined by the Rent Officer; different criteria apply. In an extreme case, the reasonable rent procedure may be useful for determining revised levels of rent, but if relations between landlord and tenant are in such a state that the rent cannot be determined amicably without reference to a third party, it may be time for the tenant to move or the landlord to evict. In Chapter 4 I discussed the matter of a reasonable rent and suggested that at the start of a contract a market rent should be set, and that it should thereafter rise annually at the rate of inflation or less. Rent tribunals will probably not follow this formula, but it seems an acceptable basis for an amicable agreement between sharers.

TAX AND MORTGAGE IMPLICATIONS

Most mortgage agreements contain clauses which prohibit letting. This is very much to be regretted. The owner of a mortgaged property who wishes to share is faced with two options. The first is to take in tenants, in breach of the mortgage agreement, and withhold the information from the mortgagee. This is probably the simplest course of action. Few mortgagees will complain about this, provided that the mortgage payments are kept up to date. Indeed, there is no reason why the mortgagees need ever know. The method is rather risky, as in law the mortgagee could demand immediate repayment of the principal amount together with any arrears of interest.

There is a very good reason for these clauses. If for any

reason the tenants were to obtain security of tenure, the market value of the property and therefore the security for the mortgagee's loan would be significantly reduced. In practice, under the present law, security of tenure could be established only if the owner were non-resident: for example, if he or she went to live abroad for a period and had not made a suitably worded tenancy agreement. If the owner were then to default on the mortgage payments, the mortgagee would want to sell the property to recover the loan, but could find it difficult to evict the sitting tenants. The property would be sold, probably at auction, and would realize perhaps only 60-70 per cent of the vacant possession price. In practice, the mortgagee can usually claim vacant possession if the mortgagor has not informed him of the tenancy, which could be hard on the tenants.

The second option open to the owner who wishes to share his or her property is to declare the intention to the mortgagee. The mortgagee should in theory agree to waive the clause prohibiting letting; but not all mortgagees will do so, and if the owner were then to go ahead and let regardless he would be placing the whole mortgage at risk.

A more reasonable clause would be one which prevented letting of the whole of the property, but which permitted non-exclusive licenses to be granted for the use of part of the property, provided always that the mortgagor notified the mortgagee each time such a license was granted, and if necessary gave the mortgagee the right to veto any agreement which was in his opinion unsatisfactory.

On balance, the first option involves less overall risk. There is, however, another very bad reason why owners tend to take the first option.

Tax

Rental income is subject to tax. If the rent is paid in cash, and the mortgagee is not told about it, there is no need to tell the Inland Revenue about it. This attitude is taken by many owners. Funnily enough, these owners are usually the ones who have a very satisfactory income from other sources. Tax fraud is the commonest 'white collar' crime and is considered almost respectable, so much so that the criminals who commit it are often stalwarts of the local Neighbourhood Watch scheme, and are strong proponents of Law and Order. There is a nasty smell of humbug around.

Not paying what you are by law required to pay is a crime, but paying what you need not pay is folly. Sensible tax management is essential, and it may be possible for almost all your rental income to be offset against appropriate expenditure so that in the end very little tax has to be paid. Income tax law is extremely complicated, and it is beyond the scope of this book to give anything but the most basic advice. Much help is available free from your local tax office on matters of law, but it cannot advise you how to reduce your tax bill overall. For this you should consult your accountant.

Income tax is payable on income. Income is classified by the Revenue into various schedules, identified by letters of the alphabet. Schedule A, for example, denotes income from land; Schedule D refers to the profits of a trade or business, and Schedule E is salaries and wages received in the course of employment. Schedule D applies to self-employed people, while Schedule E is for employed people and tax on Schedule E income is collected under PAYE.

Rental income is Schedule A income. Before the early 1960s all owner-occupiers paid tax on the imputed rent from their property, the argument being that if they did not live in the property they would receive rental income from the tenants, which would be taxable, and would pay rent for the place where they did live out of their general taxed income. Tax on imputed Schedule A income makes sense, unlike most income tax legislation, but it was extremely unpopular. However, mortgage interest payments could be deducted from the imputed rent, so the full impact of the tax only hit those who had paid off their mortgages, or those whose repayment mortgages were nearing the end of their term. Reginald Maudling, who was then Chancellor of the Exchequer, abolished the imputed Schedule A income, but he continued to allow mortgage interest to be offset against other income. Tax relief on mortgage interest may still be claimed on the first £30,000 of a mortgage.

The principle of tax schedules allows appropriate expenditure to be offset against income in each schedule, but not against other income. You can offset telephone expenses against Schedule D income, for the telephone costs associated with your business, but you can't offset telephone costs against your Schedule E income. For Schedule A, you can only offset expenses directly associated with the property, which primarily means repairs and maintenance. You would also have to apportion these expenses, where they applied to the whole property. Maintenance of the whole exterior of the property affects everyone who lives there.

INSURANCE

Insurance companies are particularly loth to recognize the shared house. Many companies simply won't provide cover. Those that do often impose impossible conditions.

Here are some examples of conditions imposed by insurance companies:

(1) Keys to the building should be available only to the insured, spouse and immediate family.

(2) Cover extends only to items kept in individual bedrooms, with lockable doors kept locked at all times.

The fears prompting these conditions are reasonable, even if the logic is not. In the end, you will find that while no insurance company will provide larceny cover burglary cover is obtainable. (Larceny is theft that does not involve breaking and entering; if you leave your back door open and someone walks in and takes your video, you will not be covered. If, on the other hand, damage is caused at the time of entry, you will be covered.)

You cannot afford to ignore the terms and conditions

of your insurance policy. If you take out an ordinary insurance policy and you have not told the insurers that you have lodgers you won't be covered and you would be better off not paying the premiums. Even for a small burglary claim the insurers will need a police report and the names of the lodgers may well come out in that. And even if, in these circumstances, the insurers were to pay out, if they later discovered that you had had lodgers at the time they would be entitled to sue you for the money paid out in error. No insurance company can be asked to take on a risk when some of the material facts are being withheld from it. The reason insurance companies won't give larceny cover to shared houses is that they assume lodgers could be tempted to make off with the boodle and pass it to an accommodating fence, whereas members of a family are more likely to respect the property of other members. In these days of smack-taking youngsters ready to take their own mother's widow's pension for a fix, such an assumption is dubious.

In the end, you will have to accept a costlier and less comprehensive insurance policy as the price of living in a share. Insurance companies will not provide communal insurance, either, although they do accept joint insurance proposals from two people.

Insurance of the building is the responsibility of the landlord, and the cost should be met out of the rent. The landlord may also insure the furniture and fittings against fire and flood, which should come out of the rent.

As landlord, you may also wish to take out some kind of liability insurance, to provide cover in the unlikely event that one of your lodgers should sue you for negligence. For example, if your lodger fell downstairs and broke his neck because you had neglected to nail down the carpet properly, you might well be liable for very considerable damages. The risks in this kind of insurance are low, as are the premiums.

It is important to have adequate cover for your belongings as your insurance company will remind you. Suppose your belongings are worth £10,000, but you have declared only £5,000 to the insurance company and are only paying the premium on £5,000 worth of insurance. You are bur-gled and goods to the value of £800 are stolen. Because you were under-insured, the company is obliged to pay out only half your claim, and you will receive only £400. Insurance companies quite frequently send out loss asses-sors, even for small claims, to check for this, particularly if the amount of your total cover seems small in relation either to your claim or to other properties of a similar type in your area.

SECURITY

Insurance companies get very paranoid about security. Given the appalling number of burglaries in cities today you would do well to be worried too.

Some houses are intrinsically vulnerable. Weak spots are tall hedges and big gardens that allow an intruder to approach the house undetected. Ground-floor windows not visible from the road – because of a tall, dense hedge for example – are particularly vulnerable.

No house can be proof against the determined pro-fessional burglar. Such thieves don't usually bother with ordinary houses, unless they know that they will find something of great value on the premises. Your worry is the casual burglar, the lads out on an afternoon job, and (sad to say) the crack or smack addicts from the nearby high-rise looking for the money for a fix. For such people, the great deterrent is the fear of being caught – the observant neighbour who will report them to the police or, worst of all, you coming home and catching them red-handed.

Terraced houses are often an easy target for an oppor-tunist burglar. Many burglars come in through the back. If you have a back alley or path, you will be particularly vulnerable. Many houses in towns don't have back alleys as the walled gardens back directly on to the walled gar-dens of the next street. Unfortunately, those back alleys that do exist are often dedicated as highways, and even if all the owners want to close them off it is not legally possible without a lengthy consultation process.

If you have a back alley, close the gate permanently

or put a very good lock on it. Be extra careful about the windows at the back. Unlike the front windows, they are relatively unobserved, and all the windows should be firmly locked. Your back door should always be locked, with the key taken out of the lock. Never leave a ladder accessible at the back.

Where there is no back alley, the problem is less severe. However, it is still possible for an athletic burglar to vault across several garden walls into your garden, so be careful and lock up.

Most burglars come in through a door – often the front door. The front door should strong, made of hardwood, and locked with a good mortice deadlock. The deadlock should conform to BS 3621. It will have a complex five-lever mechanism, and the bolt, probably made of brass, will have two hardened steel rollers in the middle. These make it very difficult to cut with a hacksaw, as they roll against the blade. In addition to the deadlock, an ordinary cylinder rimlock such as a Yale lock is useful as a latch only. It is good practice to change the locks regularly, particularly if tenants move in and out. Locks with registered keys are more expensive but the blanks for cutting duplicate keys are obtainable only from reputable locksmiths, who will only cut keys for the registered keyholder.

Advice on crime prevention can be obtained from your local police station. Most have a Crime Prevention Officer who can recommend ways of improving security.

KEYS
Keep a track of all your keyholders: it is a good idea to get keyholders to sign for the keys they are given. A spare set of keys is useful, particularly if you have guests staying, but keep track of it. Never leave keys in an unguarded place for collection. Don't leave them under the doormat, on a string behind the letterbox, under a stone in the front garden, behind the porch light, above the door lintel, in the old house-martins' nest in the porch. If you must send them through the post, make sure that there is no reference to the address in or on the letter or

anywhere else. Don't mark a key-tag with an address. If a handbag is lost or stolen containing keys and address-bearing documents, change the locks immediately. Keep a spare Yale cylinder in the house with sufficient keys for this purpose (changing the cylinder takes ten minutes). Don't take risks with keys.

Front windows should be kept locked. Fit window locks to all of them. Ground-floor front windows should be kept permanently shut; first-floor windows may be left slightly open if fitted with locks that allow this (it is usually possible with sash windows and with the better-designed aluminium replacement windows).

Some houses have bars fitted to the inside of ground-floor windows. I think this is a horrifying trend, that we should become virtual prisoners in our own homes, defended with bars of iron. Neither am I convinced that bars deter burglars; on the contrary, they would suggest to me that the house contained something worth nicking. The main argument against these bars is that they look hideous. A better, if slightly costlier, alternative is to fit laminated glass. Laminated glass is not entirely unbreakable in the thickness normally fitted – 6.4 mm; however, thicker versions are available. If you do fit thicker glass, you may find that the glass is stronger than the window-frame. Georgian wired glass breaks as easily as ordinary glass and the wires can easily be snipped. It is *not* a security glass.

Burglar alarms are sometimes required by insurance companies. They are expensive, and you may achieve the same degree of deterrent effect from a dummy alarm bell. However, in some areas the alarm bell may simply serve to inform burglars that you have something worth protecting. If you do fit a dummy bell, make sure that no one sees you fitting it, or get a proper alarm company to fit it. If everyone knows it's a dummy, it will not be much use. The second major drawback of alarms is the complex procedure required to arm them before you leave, and the equally complex disarming process on your return, with the consequent false alarms that wake up the entire neighbourhood. It might be assumed that the procedures could be simplified without compromising security, but the alarm companies have not so far managed to achieve this.

If you're out in the evenings, leave a light on in the sitting room (not the hall) visible from the road, but make sure the curtains or blinds are closed. As an added precaution, it's a good idea to leave the radio or the television on as well, particularly on a channel with a lot of talking. Few things deter a burglar more than the sound of voices.

If you're going away for a while, cancel the milk and ask the neighbours to keep an eye on the property. There's an argument in favour of cancelling the papers, but if both the milkman and the paper boy know you're away there's no reason why they shouldn't tell their mates, who might just possibly be interested in a spot of burglary. If you're away for any length of time, a house sitter is a good idea – a reliable friend who can stay in the house and thus deter intruders. However, in most shared houses this problem doesn't arise. The only time the whole house is likely to be away is at Christmas; in the summer, everyone normally staggers their holidays. Student houses always have the vacations to contend with, but usually someone will stay up for the Easter vac and for the long vac the house is usually given up in any case.

CHAPTER 6

Eating together

Many flatsharers do not bother with communal meals. Instead, everyone has their own store cupboard, and people put bossy little labels over things in the fridge. Milk, tea and coffee may be regarded as communal property, but even these tend to be bought individually, and tea and coffee made for others as a courtesy rather than as part of the overall routine of the house.

The excuse given for such a system is that since everyone comes in at different times, no one knows who's gong to be in and everyone likes to lead free and easy lives, no other system is practical. This is almost always a load of tosh. With a bit of organization, a communal meal system can be made to work very well. The advantages of communal meals usually outweigh any possible disadvantages.

Many people are put off communal meals by bad experiences in the past, perhaps of Earnest Regiments – houses where the daily routine is strictly Stalinist, and life in general and meals in particular are subject to the control of the Big Brother notice board in the kitchen. Woe betide anyone in such a house who fails to cook on their allotted day.

Others are just looking for freedom, after years of Mum's cooking at home ('We'll be having tea at seven, dear. You will try to be back in time, won't you? You know how your father hates it when you're late. . .'); the joy of not having to be back at specified times is intoxicating at first.

All too often the temptation is just to get a take-away on the way home. You're tired and hungry, and can't be bothered to cook a proper meal. A bag of chips, a kebab – such foul food tastes delectable when you're starving. Or perhaps you go for a can of ravioli – I have even known people whose staple diet was *cold* canned ravioli, which must be the ultimate in revolting convenience food. The next time you go home, of course, Mum will say to you, 'I do hope you're eating properly. You don't look well at all . . .' And you know that the reason you don't look well is that you have been out till one every night for the last week, working hard and living hard, giving your liver a real battering, but the pleasure of tasting fresh vegetables at dinner makes you realize what you've been missing.

However hard you try to be virtuous by sticking to yoghurt and granary bread sandwiches at lunchtime, stuffing yourself with junk every evening will ultimately tell on your health. This does not mean you have to have meat and two vegetables for dinner each night, but you should aim for a well-balanced diet high in protein, fibre and vitamins. It is much easier to eat a balanced meal at home than it is to buy one at a restaurant. Much fast food contains a high proportion of fat, sugar and salt. At home you can control your intake of those items, and make sure you eat fresh fruit and vegetables regularly.

One of the greatest advantages of a shared house is that it makes it easy to have proper meals, more often than not. Of course, there will always be days when nobody wants to cook and when the easiest course of action is to dial for a pizza or run to the end of the road for a Chinese take-away, but even then eating communally is much cheaper – and more interesting – than eating singly.

At home, cooking a meal for five is as easy as cooking a meal for one; and the food will usually cost much less than five times the cost of a meal for one. You can, with a clear conscience, cook only one day a week and yet eat a proper meal every week night. However, eating communally will need to be organized and some kind of system established to make things fair.

In our house, we have a meals chart, a sheet of paper

attached to a clipboard in the back room. As there are
five of us, each day on the chart is divided into six boxes
– one for each person and one for the cook. From time to
time everyone in the house checks his or her diary and
fills in the days ahead. Each member of the household
decides which will be the most convenient day for him
or her to cook, and writes his or her name or initial in the
'cook' box for that particular day. For the other days of
the week, there's a choice of 'in', 'out' or 'late'. We have
supper, in theory at least, at eight, so anyone anticipating
a return home much after eight will put an L in his or
her box for the day in question. If anyone's movements
are uncertain, the box is left blank. In practice, over a
period of four years, we have found that the system runs
better in winter than in summer, simply because most of
us are out more in the long summer evenings. In student
houses the system can really come into its own in the last
few weeks before finals – better to break from the books
for a proper meal than for the whole house to sneak off
to the Union bar for stale pie and several pints.

If you run a system like ours, on the day you've chosen to cook you check the meals chart in the morning.
If you're planning to cook something like pork chops,
for which portions and numbers are fairly crucial, you'll
check whether there are any blanks for that day (and if
there *are* any you'll try to ask the ditherers to make up
their minds before it's too late). You'll also check the store
cupboards for your ingredients, and do your shopping on
the way home, or whenever suits. You write what you've
spent on a little docket and put it in the dockets box (see
Chapter 4), to keep the household accounting system
straight. You get home at a reasonable time, rustle up
your culinary masterpiece, dish it up, then sit down
and relax. The rule is that the cook never washes up
– although it helps domestic harmony if you can do
some of the clearing up in the kitchen as you go along
so that those who do get to wash up aren't faced with
total mayhem in the kitchen.

For the purposes of the household accounts, the total
amount spent on food is divided by the total number of

meals eaten to arrive at a price per meal, and when the
accounts are done everyone gets charged for the number
of meals eaten according to the signing-in chart.

The system is splendidly flexible. No need to commit yourself until the last minute; no need to set aside
every Thursday because that's your night to cook. Nor
is there any compulsion to cook for a certain number
of nights: one chap who lived with us for a long time
cooked barely thrice in the best part of three years, but
he did the washing up nearly every night. (He was a very
good cook, but he was supposed to be studying for his
accountancy exams and this way he could work in his
room until the meal was ready.)

If you're going to be back late, a meal can be kept
for you, and if you're unexpectedly delayed a call to the
cook can cancel your meal or have it kept for you to eat
later. Even if you're out, having said that you would be
in, the only penalty is the cost of the meal, which hardly
breaks the bank.

What if you work shifts?
People who work flexible shifts, such as nurses, are
well suited to the above-described meals system. On
late shifts, the food can be kept until they get home;
on earlies, they have a free afternoon to do some relatively relaxed shopping and cook a meal for everyone.
Journalists, actors and others working irregular hours are
a bit harder to reconcile to a system geared to a house
of nine-to-fivers, not least because the appeal of eating
re-heated or kept-hot dinners frequently is rather limited.
On days off, however, such people can participate, and
during the week they will no doubt rely on canteens and
the like. The system is flexible enough to accommodate
even someone who eats only two communal meals a year.

How communal should food be?
There should be no 'no-go' areas in the kitchen (the
fridge, the food cupboard), and there must be a total
ban on bossy little notices – anywhere in the house, not
simply the kitchen. The rule applies with extra strength

in the fridge, so everything is fair game for nibbles all the time. Anyone who buys a quarter of olives or a pound of cheese will realize that these items are fair game, and accordingly charge them to the docket system. It would be a bit off, however, to charge the ingredients for a private self-indulgent pig-out to the system, and you probably wouldn't want anyone to know about that comforting but guilt-inspiring Marathon bar, would you?

Bread, butter or polyunsaturated margarine, milk and cereal are kept for people to have a snack as necessary. The hungry can have a piece of toast and jam with a cup of tea, and there's a biscuit tin which from time to time is filled with gingernuts for just such a purpose. Tea, coffee and cocoa are also part of the communal system. Our household revolves round tea. Made in a pot, it is a much more sociable drink than instant coffee made in a mug.

SHOPPING

Picking up odd items from the corner shop every day isn't a very cost-effective way of buying food. It's better to go to a big supermarket about once a month and stock up on staples. If you have a car, this kind of shopping trip is quite painless apart from the brief moment at the check-out when you pay the bill. Without a car, you have the problem of carrying everything home. There is only one sensible solution to this, which is to get a shopping trolley. For some reason or other, shopping trolleys are considered naff, except perhaps when used by elderly ladies, but when the alternative is to have your arms wrenched from their sockets, who cares? Go for the most capacious trolley you can find, and pay no attention to the jibes of your friends. I must admit it took a slipped disc to persuade me to buy one, but when I think back to the struggles I had with shopping in the past I can't think why I didn't buy one earlier. The only time a trolley seems really stupid is on the way to the shops, when it makes a terrible noise over the paving stones – for some reason, it's quieter when it's full. One of my flatmates is so concerned about this that she carries the trolley to the shops, but whether this is even more stupid is a moot point.

The shopping trolley is also very useful for trips to your local market. Supermarket fruit and vegetables are grossly overpriced, although the differentials are falling. My local supermarket has a rule of thumb for sweet peppers: it charges the same price for *one* as the market charges for a *pound* – and there are usually four peppers to a pound (weight). Five years ago, you could have been sure of better choice and quality at the market but the big branches of the main stores – the superstores and hypermarkets – now offer a very good range of produce; the market wins on price and when it comes to atmosphere and fun there is no contest.

MILK AND BREAD

The best way to get milk is from your milkman, delivered to your doorstep every day. Unfortunately, many milkmen have taken to delivering mid-morning rather than early morning, and as a result the dairies are complaining that more people now buy milk from the supermarket. I cannot believe this crass stupidity, which stems in no small part to the persistence of the dairy managers' belief in the nuclear family. Households where *everyone* goes out to work prefer to have their milk delivered before 8 o'clock in the morning – and can afford to pay a penny or two more for a pint than the supermarket charges. 'Housewives' – or anyone who is at home when the milkman comes – also have the time, and the motivation, to go down the road to the supermarket for cheaper milk. So come on, dairymen: consumers will happily pay for a delivery service, if it's reasonably early – but if the milk is going to sit on the doorstep all day long and go sour in the summer (or, more likely, get nicked) we'll go to the supermarket instead and put you out of business.

We still haven't come up with a satisfactory solution to the bread problem. Quite apart from the extreme difficulty of obtaining good bread and the prevalence of truly yucky pap at many so-called 'traditional' bakers, we never seem to get the co-ordination right. Either nobody buys bread, or three people do, so we end up with two stale and mouldy loaves. The best arrangement is for the cook to be responsible for replenishing the bread stock if necessary: but even this doesn't address the fact that the bread disappears most quickly on the days when no one is cooking.

DRINK

Drink has always tended to cause upsets in shared houses, because it's so expensive. The answer – which, unfortunately, is easier to recommend than to carry out – is not to get uptight about it. We have a communal drinks cupboard, but we also have an unwritten (and unspoken) rule that its contents are not for getting drunk on. Occasionally we have a communal getting-drunk session when we go out and buy a few cans of Crucial Brew; and sometimes the contents of the cupboard are raided late at night to smooth the path of a seduction or for some other reason; but in this case the consumer always buys a replacement.

Medical experts are now generally of the opinion that most people drink too much alcohol, and, quite apart from the dangers of drinking and driving, even relatively small quantities of alcohol drunk regularly can cause long-term damage to the liver and increase the risk of obesity, heart disease and ulcers. Tea is the answer. A habitual gin and tonic, or glass of sherry, or can of beer, as an unwinder when you get in is very nice but if you have one every night, plus the odd night out, before very long you will be consuming rather more alcohol than is good for you. Tea may not seem quite so decadent, or so appealing, but a freshly-made pot of tea is just as effective as an unwinder, in a different sort of way. (Tea may not have a completely clean bill of health, but by any standards it is a lot less bad for you than alcohol.) Once the tea habit has become entrenched, you can be more relaxed about alcohol. Keep the gin and tonic for a treat – on Friday nights or at weekends.

In our house, gin is a communal item bought on our trips to the supermarket. We don't, by and large, drink on our own, but together as a household. We also have an unwritten rule that those who go abroad, for work or play, come back with a bottle of duty-free spirit. By this means we manage to have a choice of malt whisky, good-quality rum, Calvados and cognac most of the time. When we're feeling particularly in need of a lift, small glasses of spirits accompany our bedtime cocoa.

Wine and beer are not usually charged to the docket system. From time to time a bottle of wine or six cans of beer will be contributed to a meal by someone feeling generous. The exception to this is home-brew, which we make from time to time; this sits in the cellar and allows us to enjoy the odd beer with a meal without feeling guilty about the cost.

CHAPTER 7

Cooking

Cooking happens to be very easy. However, some people develop hopeless complexes about it. In many families, cooking is done so exclusively by Mum that everyone feels as though some arcane science is being practised, with knowledge and secrets that can only be acquired with years of practice and training at the apron-strings of a potent Earth Goddess.

This is nonsense. *Everyone* can cook. There is no need to resort to packet mixes and take-aways just because you've been sent out into the big wide world. Ignorance of food is the main problem. I once shared a flat with two women. On Shrove Tuesday, one of them decided we should have pancakes and so in preparation for it all she bought a packet of pancake mix for about 30 pence. 'Easy!' proclaimed the packet. 'Just add milk and an egg!' Now as pancakes consist of *only* flour, milk and an egg 30p seemed an awful lot to pay for about three tablespoonfuls of flour – which we would have had in stock anyway. However, in all fairness I should mention that although the main ingredient of the mix was certainly flour, it also contained a large number of additives with long names, the purpose of which was apparently to bulk out the ingredients declaration.

Pancakes are not an isolated example: there are many more fairly basic dishes and sauces sold in packets, cans and sachets which can be made from scratch at a fraction of the cost, very little more effort and not a great deal more time.

Be that as it may, there is a type of cooking which tends to predominate in shared houses, based on the tuna fish/pasta/sweetcorn/mince axis: Tuna fish salad, lasagne, spaghetti bolognese and chilli con carne may be excellent when done well, but they are often *not* done well. Nor is there any need to limit your menus to this repertoire.

Doing justice to your ingredients and varying your diet are not the only important criteria where cooking is concerned, however. Meals should also be cheap, nutritious, filling and, above all, taste good.

This is not a cookbook, but the following hints on cooking and food preparation, plus a selection of easy recipes and shopping guides, may be useful to those who feel that they really can't cook and therefore need a safety net if they are ever to take the plunge.

The science of cookery is largely a matter of knowing your ingredients and what happens to them as you cook them. The art of cookery is combining the flavours, colours and textures of your ingredients to create a successful dish.

VEGETABLES

Vegetables are the key to eating well. We go to our local market about once a week and buy a stock of vegetables – potatoes, onions, carrots, leeks, celery, cabbage and so on. Most vegetables keep well in the fridge, and less well out of it. Potatoes need to be kept in the dark, though not in the fridge. Onions keep well out of the fridge, but carrots tend to shrivel quickly. Onions and garlic are essential flavourings for most savoury food; in vegetarian dishes they become even more important, adding a depth and richness of flavour.

Onions

Onions come in three sizes – Spanish, English and Pickling. Spanish onions don't keep quite as well as English onions, but you have to do less peeling to come up with the same amount of onion. I don't think they taste as nice as English ones, either, and they are about 25 per cent more expensive.

Peeling and chopping Don't believe there are tricks to stop you crying. Glasses help, and the best bet would probably be a snorkel and face mask. Otherwise, be quick. You will become immune to the fumes after about 15 or 20 onions. You need a cutting board and a sharp knife. First of all, cut the onion in half through the top – the North Pole – and the root – the South Pole – along a line of longitude without peeling. Then peel one half at a time. Cut off the top, peel back the skin to the root but leave the root on.

Dicing and chopping First make a series of parallel cuts at right angles both to the plane of the equator and to the plane of the halving cut, going almost but not quite to the root so that the root holds everything together. Now make a series of cuts along lines of latitude. The half onion will fall into dice.

Slicing and making matchsticks Cut the root off and slice the onion through with a series of parallel cuts at right angles both to the plane of the equator and to the plane of the halving cut.

Garlic
Garlic is very potent when raw, but once cooked it loses much of its pungency and becomes rich and aromatic. Really foul garlicky breath comes from eating it raw or not well cooked – in dishes such as garlic bread or aïoli. Try to avoid these really garlicky dishes if you have a top-level meeting with valued clients the next day.

The best garlic is fresh, and firm and white or purple; beware of dusty grey marks. The taste and effect of garlic varies depending on whether it's chopped or crushed. I prefer it sliced and chopped to a purée, but others swear by a crusher. Using a knife, crack open the cloves of garlic which comprise the bulb by pressing them with the side of the knife. The skin falls away easily. You can then chop it and slice it easily, or put it in the abominable crusher.

To remove the smell of garlic or onions from your

fingers, rub salt into them before washing in soap and water.

Carrots
Carrots can be eaten whole or peeled or scraped. The easiest way to peel them is with a wobbly peeler. Peeled carrots have the best appearance but you lose some of the vitamins which are concentrated in the skin. Scraped carrots tend to go a bit spongy on the outside. The inside of the carrots – the yellow core – can get a bit woody in old carrots. If you're using old carrots in a salad in winter, grate them lengthways and leave the yellow core behind. Carrots add a pleasant sweetness to soups and stews.

Leeks
Leeks get mucky. If you're going to eat them whole, peel off the outer leaves, cut the leeks to the length you intend, and stand them upside down in a jug of water for a few hours so that the muck falls to the bottom. If not, slice them half through *lengthways* before washing them. Leeks are delicious in winter soups. In the summer you can boil them whole, press out as much of the water as you can and then serve them cold – or warm – with a vinaigrette dressing.

Mushrooms
Mushrooms don't keep very well; they last better in the fridge than out of it. The tops are tenderer than the stalks. A quick good wash cleans them well; there's no need to peel them. Mushrooms add richness and a dark colour to vegetable dishes.

Sweet peppers
For years these only came in two varieties, green and red according to their ripeness. Then came yellow peppers, which two years ago were three or four times the price of the red and the green and available only in specialist markets on a good day when the moon was right. Now you can get yellow, red and green peppers everywhere. I'm not convinced that the taste varies much, and I get

the impression that all peppers are now much blander than they once were. However, they are tasty, crisp and pretty in a salad. Peppers also add some aromatic flavour to stews, but all lose their bright colour with extended cooking. Sweet peppers are related to chilli peppers and the seeds can be a bit hot.

Tomatoes
The best tomatoes for cooking are the canned Italian tomatoes, which have more flavour than the ordinary round tomatoes sold fresh in the markets. Chopped tomatoes are better value than whole peeled tomatoes. Tomato purée comes in a tube; the cans and jars are only very marginally cheaper and once opened the contents quickly go mouldy. Fresh tomatoes are for salads, for having stuffed, for cutting in half and grilling for Sunday breakfast. Most fresh tomatoes taste rather dull, but recently cherry tomatoes have been sporadically available. These are delicious in salads, particularly if peeled and dressed with a sprinkling of tarragon vinegar, sea salt and chopped chives. Fresh plum tomatoes and giant-size 'beefsteak' tomatoes are also now seen on sale from time to time.

To peel tomatoes, put a pan of water on the fire, bring to a rolling boil, drop your tomatoes in, one or two at a time, and leave for exactly ten seconds; remove and peel: the skin comes away easily. This is a much better way than holding them over a gas flame on a fork; if you do embark on the gas-flame method sooner or later you will end up wishing you'd boiled the pan of water instead.

Potatoes
Potatoes are the king of vegetables. They are cheap and keep fairly well but must be kept in the dark, otherwise they go green, when they are bitter and slightly poisonous.

Baked potatoes are a simple, popular and reliable dish. You need a hot oven, 220°C/425°F/Gas 7. If the oven is only at Gas 5 or so, they will not cook at all. Speared with skewers or potato bakers, a 6-8 oz potato (enough for one person) will cook in approximately 40 minutes. Unspeared, it will take 1 hour 20 minutes.

Boiled potatoes don't take long (10 minutes, roughly, depending on how small they are cut). Put them in cold salted water and bring to the boil, following the universal vegetable cooking rule that things growing below the ground go in cold water, things growing above the ground in boiling water. Test them with the point of a knife until they are done.

The potato has a delicious texture, but if you want to mash yours at least it will taste much better than packet mash. Boil and drain the potatoes, put them back in the pot on the hob for a moment to dry through, then add milk, butter, pepper and nutmeg. For an interesting variation, replace the butter with olive oil and mix in some chopped chives.

Instant mash is useful as a thickener for stews and soups; it is heartier than arrowroot and less gluey than cornflour or flour. Be sure to get the powdered version. 'Potato nuggets' are completely useless for anything other than mash.

For *gratin dauphinoise*, cook sliced potatoes in milk and (optionally) cheese in the oven; they take forever unless you make sure that the whole mixture is boiling. The best way is to bring the dish to the boil on the hob, in a fireproof (metal or flameproof earthenware) dish, before putting them in the oven.

Pulses

Lentils may be the butt of every hippy joke, but pulses are very useful for cheap, nutritious food. Pulses absorb the flavours of spices and seasonings very well; they also – if vegetarians will forgive the heresy – combine excellently with small amounts of meat. Dried pulses are far cheaper than the canned ones and there is no need to shy away from them simply because they need a little forethought before use in dishes.

Not all pulses need to be soaked, and even those that do need soaking will usually be all right if put to soak in the morning for an evening meal. By and large pulses taste bland on their own and need enlivening with seasonings. One of the best pulses is the butter bean (which *does* need soaking) but you'd be surprised how many people have a horror of them after having had to eat them in school meals, served entirely without seasoning.

Although meat is an excellent 'flavouring' for pulses, vegetarians eat pulses for the protein they provide. From that point of view adding meat is a cop-out. The best vegetarian way of seasoning pulses is with herbs and spices; the Indians have been doing it for centuries and the huge variety of dall recipes is an object lesson in how to make pulses really tasty.

The bigger the bean, the longer the soaking and cooking times. All dry pulses must be boiled for a minimum of 10 minutes after soaking, and the initial water must be discarded.

Pulses contain a lot of fibre, which is good news, but they also contain some oligosaccharides, which create wind. If you soak and rinse the pulses you will remove some of these oligosaccharides, which ease the wind problem. Some spices, notably ginger but also caraway seeds and cumin seeds, are carminatives and therefore help reduce the wind problem.

Grains
Grains complement the proteins in pulses. All meatless meals, and vegan meals in particular, which exclude both meat and dairy produce, must be balanced – that is, both grains and pulses should be eaten at the same meal. Always use the whole grain, because it has the best flavour and the highest nutritional value. Suitable grains include rice, wheat, oats and barley.

Rice feeds half the world. The five varieties you are most likely to come across are basmati, brown, pre-fluffed, patna and pudding (short-grain). A sixth, Italian Arborio, can usually be bought only from delicatessens, but is essential for real risotto. Basmati, which is the ideal rice for Indian dishes but is more expensive than other kinds, has a very long grain, cooks easily, and is

delicious. Some so-called basmati contains a high proportion of inferior rice; Tilda is a reliable brand. Brown,
or wholegrain rice, should be your staple. It contains all
the vitamins, protein and natural oils that make rice so
nutritious. It also takes longer to cook than other kinds
(about 30 minutes). You can also get brown basmati and
brown pre-fluffed rice. Pre-fluffed rice, of which Uncle
Ben's is the main example, is rice which has been treated
to make it easy to cook. Follow the instructions on the
packet. Patna rice is ordinary, white, long-grain rice. It
varies in quality enormously, and the cheapest has a lot
of broken grains which make it impossible to cook well.
Even the best patna needs very careful cooking if it is to
come out dry and fluffy.

Pudding rice is round-grained rice from Carolina, and is
for making rice pudding and other dessert dishes. Thirty
years ago the only rice most shops stocked was pudding
rice and cookery books featured large notices about being
sure to get long-grain rice for savoury cooking. So great
has the change been in our eating habits over the last
two-and-a-half decades that you now have to look quite
hard for pudding rice.

There are two main methods for cooking rice – the
absorption method and the surplus water method. For
the surplus water method, boil a large pan of water, add
salt, and when the water is boiling add the rice. Use at
least six cups of water to each one of rice: a cup of rice
provides roughly 2-3 portions. Test the rice after seven
minutes (longer for brown rice). It is just done when you
can bite a grain without finding a hard, crunchy bit in
the middle. Drain the rice and rinse well with cold water.
Finally, rinse again with hot water and keep warm.

For the absorption method you need exactly the right
amount of water, which is all absorbed. You can therefore use stock or milk instead of water, allowing the rice
to absorb the flavour. Use $1^1/_2$-$2^1/_2$ cups of liquid to every
cup of rice; the exact amount depends on the rice, and
with practice you will be able to judge the amount of
liquid to add fairly accurately. Start with too little liquid
rather than too much. Wash the rice well before you put

it into the pan. If you find you have too much liquid left when the rice is cooked, boil hard for a minute or so, watching constantly to make sure it does not burn. For fried or pilau rice, start by frying the rice in oil, perhaps with onions and spices, before adding the liquid. Boil, then turn the heat down low. For best results, put the dish in the oven at this stage.

Bread Wheat is the traditional staple grain of Europe, eaten as a staple in the form of pasta, bread and pastry, all of which are made from flour. Wholemeal flour is made from the whole grain, including bran; white flour has had the most nutritious part of the grain refined out of it. Wholemeal flour is therefore better for you than white flour.

Bread is the form in which people in the West eat most wheat. Don't forget that you can use it as the basic carbohydrate component of a meal – chunks of wholemeal bread are as good as baked potatoes with a stew, for example. Otherwise, bread is a convenience food, a slice of toast or a sandwich providing the ideal stop-gap. Unless you have all day and a large country kitchen it is seldom worth while making bread at home.

Pasta A mainstay of shared-house cooking, pasta is inexpensive and both quick and easy to cook. Try eating it as they do in Italy – as a first course rather than a main course. Italians eat at least as much pasta for their first courses as non-Italians do when they have it as a main course; having filled up on carbohydrate (the pasta, which is cheap), they want only a very little (expensive) meat afterwards. Pasta makes a little sauce go a long, long way. Sauces can be made from meat, vegetables or dairy products, but unless you are on a diet it's worth putting a little more oil or butter in the sauce than you might if you were to eat the sauce on its own; with the pasta, it won't seem at all greasy. Wholemeal pasta is good, but it has a distinctive nutty flavour which needs a robust

sauce to complement it. Delicate sauces, such as pesto
or carbonara, are better with white pasta.

Pastry Occasionally you may make pastry at home, for
pies or quiches. Wholemeal pastry is fashionable but in
my opinion it is a waste of time. Pastry is not exactly a
healthy food, as it has to be made with saturated fats. If
health is your main concern, you shouldn't eat pastry of
any description. Gastronomically, wholemeal pastry can
be good in earthy, hearty dishes, such as pasties, but is an
abomination in delicate flans and quiches. Frozen pastry
is quite good, but it is never made with butter, which is
a shame, since pastry – particularly puff pastry – made
with butter only is scrumptious.

Oats Whole oats, called groats, can be cooked a bit like
rice. They are very high in protein. The best porridge is
made from medium oatmeal rather than porridge oats –
which, however, are good for flapjacks. Medium oatmeal
is a good coating agent instead of breadcrumbs for fried
food, and makes a crunchy crumble topping.

Barley The two main types available are pearl barley,
which is polished like white rice, and pot barley, which
is the whole grain. Health food stores sell it; at about 25p
a pound, compared with rice at 50-60p a pound, barley is
very cheap. This is because rice is subject to EC duties.
Use barley as you would rice; it takes about 30-40 minutes
to cook and makes a nutritious and cheap alternative with
a delicious chewy texture. Pot barley tastes much better
(and is healthier, for it contains more fibre) than pearl
barley, but is a little harder to obtain. Barley is cooked
in the same way as rice, by either the absorption method
or the surplus water method. Cooking time isn't critical,
however: the result will just be more or less chewy
according to the time allowed.

Cheese

Cheese is another useful staple. It is expensive as a convenient nibble (not to mention fattening and otherwise bad for you), but as a cooking ingredient it's very useful. Cheddar is a popular choice for cooking, but the best English cheese for cooking is Lancashire. In fact, you can use almost any cheese in cooking: the results may vary, but are usually interesting. Toasted cheese sandwiches are a favourite snack, but I think that they're better with a few embellishments. Toasted Cheddar and apple are good; toasted Brie with spring onions and sliced green chillis, the whole sprinkled with lime or lemon juice when cooked, is also worth a try.

Meat

Meat doesn't keep unless it's frozen. Use it within a day or two of buying it. As a general rule, the tougher it is, the less it costs. Tough meat can be made more tender, and all meat is improved, by marinating. The British tend not to include marinating in their traditional culinary repertoire, except where venison is concerned, since they reckon their meat is tender enough; moreover, it has always been cold enough for most of the meat to become tender through hanging, while in warmer climates it has had to be preserved by marinating. Marinating simply means soaking in a marinade, an acid liquid together with some seasonings. The acidity helps to tenderize and preserve the meat, and the seasonings improve the flavour, while most of the tenderizing is done by natural enzymes in the meat.

When cooking meat, there are two basic rules. The first is that fierce heat toughens meat, and the second is that if meat is quickly browned to 'seal' it before cooking, it will taste good. To brown meat, expose it to a high heat in order to caramelize the sugars in the meat juices. Grilled or roast meat goes brown naturally during the cooking, but meat for a stew must first be browned in a frying-pan (shut the kitchen door and open the windows while you do this, unless you're lucky enough to have an extractor hood, as it creates a lot of smoke and a strong smell). Even mince is worth browning properly; and when it has been browned, you won't need to add gravy browning or any other colouring agent. The browning toughens the meat, but when it is then cooked slowly in a liquid for a long time, it becomes tender again.

Pork and bacon Pork, a white meat, also benefits from the treatment described above.

Bacon is a very useful standby in a shared kitchen, mainly because it keeps quite well in the fridge. A few rashers of bacon chopped up can form the basis of a number of pasta sauces, and bacon sandwiches are quick and easy to make either for Saturday breakfast or as a late-night snack when the whole house has just returned from an evening's drinking.

Poultry Poultry meat is usually tender. Don't overcook poultry; it becomes slimy and stringy. If you put chicken into a casserole it's best to use only the leg and thigh meat; the breast gets very dry. Remove skin before you casserole chicken: delicious though it may be on roast or fried chicken, it's slimy (and just as fattening) on wet chicken.

You can buy chicken cut into bits. Breast meat is tender but dry and needs very little cooking, while leg and thigh meat is moister, and takes quite a bit longer to cook.

Other poultry Duck is tastier and much, much fattier than chicken. You need much more duck to feed one person (say, one bird between two people); therefore it is a luxury item. Turkey is rather dull and very dry; I have never understood how it is that we are supposed to regard it as a treat at Christmas. However, it can be cheap and sometimes bits are available at bargain prices. Usually these are tough old legs and wings as the breast has been sold off on its own to a restaurant or gone to make turkey-burgers.

FOOD POISONING:
A WARNING

*Be very careful with raw poultry meat, which is often
infected with salmonella (the bacteria of which are killed
by cooking). Chicken also contains a bacterium called
Campylobacter which is implicated as a cause of stomach
ulcers.*

*Don't let raw meat touch any cooked food or any
food to be eaten raw.*

*Throw away chicken defrost juices – they are a lethal
salmonella cocktail.*

*Raw poultry flesh and juices can contaminate sur-
faces, knives, hands, cutting boards etc. Scrub them
well, with soap and scalding water, immediately after
use. Ideally, use a sanitizing cleaner or a disinfectant.*

*Food poisoning is very unpleasant. Young, healthy
people will probably only suffer a mild stomach upset,
but it can kill the old and frail.*

Offal Offal means liver, kidneys, hearts and lungs: for
most culinary purposes, just liver and kidneys. Not all
offal is cheap. Calf's liver is as expensive as best steak,
and lamb's liver is also quite dear. Ox liver and pig's
liver are cheap. Offal, particularly liver, is very rich in
nutrients and makes beautiful rich sauces and gravies,
and, particularly lamb's offal, it is easy to cook. Pig's
liver is good if stewed for a long time in a tasty sauce.
Kidneys are great for a Sunday breakfast with bacon,
eggs, sausages and mushrooms.

Fish
Fish is generally very expensive, and is getting trendier and trendier. Only oily fish caught in UK waters
(for example, mackerel, herring and sprats) are cheap,
although certain other kinds, including coley, can also
be fairly cheap.

Fish is not often fresh. Even the beautifully stocked
counters at the big branches of supermarkets tend not
to sell really fresh fish, which can be recognized by its
bright, shining eyes; cloudy or milky eyes signify old fish.

Luckily it's the mackerel, herring and sprats that you're most likely to find fresh at a fishmonger's. Preserved fish, particularly smoked fish, are good value as they are usually smoked fairly close to the port of landing.

RECIPES

SUBSTANTIAL MEALS

Vegetarian stew with barley pilaff
Serves?

7oz (200 g) chick peas
2 onions
1lb (450 g) parsnips
$^1/_2$ head celery
8 cloves garlic
1 piece fresh ginger
2 tablespoons (30 ml) sunflower oil
1 teaspoon (5 ml) black mustard seeds

1 fresh chilli
1 14-oz (397-g) can chopped tomatoes
salt
$^1/_2$ packet cream of coconut
1 tablespoon (15 ml) garam masala
fresh coriander

Pilaff:
1 onion
8 cloves
10 oz (300 g pot barley)
1 carrot
8 tablespoons (120 ml) sunflower oil

5-cm (2-inch) stick cinnamon
2 bay leaves
1 pint (600 ml) milk (optional)
1 sprig thyme

Soak the chick peas overnight in cold water. Drain and rinse, then bring to the boil in fresh water, without salt. Boil hard for 10 minutes, then leave to simmer.

Peel and slice the onions. Peel the parsnips and cut into $^3/_4$-inch (2-cm) cubes. Slice and wash the celery. Peel and chop the garlic. Chop the chilli. Grate the ginger.

For the pilaff, peel the onion and stick the cloves into it. Wash the barley in a sieve under the cold tap. Scrape the carrot and cut in half lengthways, then into thin half-circles. Heat 8 tablespoons (120 ml) oil in a pan, then add cinnamon and bay leaves. Brown quickly, then add the carrots. Stir briskly and add the barley. Add the milk, if using (otherwise add water) and make up the liquid so that the barley is covered to a depth of about an inch (2$^1/_2$ cm). Add the onion and the thyme, bring to the boil and add 1 teaspoon (5 ml) salt. Cover tightly, lower the heat and simmer.

Heat 2 tablespoons (30 ml) oil in a pan. Add the mustard seeds and let them pop, then add the ginger, chilli, parsnips, garlic, onions and celery, in quick succession. Keep the heat high and stir all the time.

As soon as the onions have begun to soften, add the drained chick peas and the tomatoes. Season with salt. Taste and adjust seasoning if necessary. Cook for 30 minutes or until the chick peas are cooked. Cut the coconut cream into cubes and add to the stew. Stir well until all the lumps have melted and blended in. Finally, add the garam masala and garnish with chopped coriander.

Serve the dish with a green salad, ideally made from cos lettuce (in summer) or, in winter, either curly endive or Belgian chicory mixed with Chinese leaves.

This dish is suitable for vegans if the milk is omitted. If you are concerned about saturated fats, leave out the coconut.

Shopping guide
Chick peas and pot barley come from health-food shops.

Vegetables, fresh chillis, ginger and coriander can be bought from markets (particularly the Asian and West Indian produce stalls), some greengrocers and most Asian shops.

Fresh thyme is available in some large supermarkets but is cheaper from markets (try the West Indian stalls). Substitute dried thyme if necessary.

Sunflower oil can be bought in supermarkets. Cream of coconut is sold by most city corner shops, in the chilled food cabinet, wherever there is a West Indian population.

Black mustard seeds and garam masala can be bought

from all Asian shops and are cheaper in 4-oz (100-g) sachets than from the spice ranges sold in fancy jars.

Sunday Supper Noodles
Serves 4

This Chinese-style dish is very quick to make and ideal for supper on Sunday nights.

1 onion	3 rashers bacon
2 cloves garlic	3 tablespoons (45 ml) sesame
1 piece ginger about 1"	oil
(2-cm) cubed	3 tablespoons (45 ml) salted
2 green chillis	black beans
8 oz (200 g) Chinese leaves	2 tablespons (30 ml) dark
1 packet instant noodles	soy sauce

Slice the onion and chop the garlic. Grate the ginger and chop the chillis. Place all these in one bowl. Cut up the Chinese leaves and place in another bowl.

Put the noodles in a pan or a bowl and pour boiling water over them.

De-rind and bone the bacon, and cut into little pieces. Put a little oil in a frying-pan or wok and add the bacon. Cook over a high heat until the bacon is crisp, then remove with a slotted spoon and set to one side.

Put the rest of the oil in the frying-pan, then add the onion mixture. Stir rapidly over a high heat. Then add the black beans, soy sauce, noodles (drained) and Chinese leaves. Finally add the crispy bacon.

Serve in little bowls and eat with chopsticks.

Shopping guide
Instant noodles, salted black beans, sesame oil and soy sauce come from Chinese grocers. The salted beans, which keep for ages in the fridge, are a useful savoury standby, as are instant noodles (not to be confused with the type of instant noodle that has a sauce sachet with it). The plain instant noodles, made either from wholemeal flour, or white flour with eggs, or spinach, come

in slabs, three to a packet. They are available from most large supermarkets or from Chinese grocers.

The other ingredients will all be available from your local market. Try to buy English bacon.

Butter beans with beef and spinach
Serves 6

8 oz (200 g) butter beans
3 onions
6 cloves garlic
1 packet frozen spinach
2 tablespoons (30 ml) sunflower oil
8 oz (200 g) minced beef
2 teaspoons (10 ml) black peppercorns, crushed
2 14-oz (397-g) cans tomatoes
salt

Soak the butter beans overnight in cold water. Drain and rinse, then put in a pan of cold water. Bring to the boil and boil hard for 15 minutes. Drain and rinse again, replace in the pan and bring to the boil. Simmer gently.

Slice the onions. Chop the garlic. Put the spinach in a pan on the heat with a little water and allow to defrost.

Put a little oil in a pan and set it on a high heat. Add the beef, a little at a time, stirring all the time to prevent sticking. When sealed, remove the beef and set to one side.

Put the rest of the oil in the pan and add the onions and garlic. Allow to soften over a gentle heat before replacing the beef and adding the black pepper, then the drained beans, the tomatoes and spinach. Remove to a casserole dish. Adjust the seasoning (add about 1 teaspoon/5 ml salt at this stage). Cook in a slow oven (about 170°C/325°F/Gas 3) for an hour or so. The longer it is cooked, the better the dish will be.

Serve with a baked potato and a salad made from yoghurt and cucumber.

BREAKFAST DISHES

Kedgeree

1lb 4oz (600 g) finnan haddock
1 pint (600 ml) milk
1 onion
3 oz butter
7 oz (200 g) basmati rice
6 size 3 eggs
black pepper
chopped parsley

Put the haddock in a flat pan, cover with the milk and simmer for 2-3 minutes. Strain off the milk, put it to one side.

For the pilaff, peel and slice the onion. Melt the butter in a large, heavy-bottomed pan. Add the onions and soften over a gentle heat. Wash the rice and add to the pan, stirring to coat all the grains in the butter. Add the milk in which the haddock was poached. Bring to the boil, cover and simmer over a very low heat for another 15-20 minutes.

Put the eggs into boiling water and boil for exactly 8 minutes. Then stand the saucepan in the sink and run the cold tap into it. Meanwhile remove the bones and skin from the fish, breaking it into flakes. When the eggs are cool, peel them (crack the shell and loosen it by rolling the egg over the worktop under the palm of your hand: it will come away easily). Cut the eggs into quarters.

Add the eggs and fish to the pan containing the rice. Mix carefully and leave for 1-2 minutes with the lid on to let the fish and eggs warm through. Grind some black pepper over the top and sprinkle with chopped parsley.

Shopping guide
All the ingredients are available from a good supermarket, but if you can't get finnan haddock use any other good-quality smoked fish. (Avoid 'golden fillets' and the garish yellow haddock sold by fishmongers.)

Porridge

medium oatmeal ($^1/_2$ mug for 3-4 servings)
salt
water

Put the oatmeal the night before to soak when you make
your bedtime cocoa. Use four times its volume of cold
water, and add a pinch of salt. Next morning bring the
pan to the boil, stirring all the time. *Et voilà* – porridge.
Eat it with milk and brown sugar or salt.

Note Don't make porridge with milk: it tends to make
it slimy.

Shopping guide
Medium oatmeal is hard to find in English supermarkets,
but most health-food stores stock it.

Bloody mary

A cure for most severe hangovers

1 small can tomato juice
juice of 1 lemon
1 teaspoon (5 ml) salt or celery salt
1 teaspoon (5 ml) worcestershire sauce
1 teaspoon (5 ml) hot pepper sauce
over-proof vodka

Shake it all together and drink.

Buck's fizz
This drink will not cure hangovers but it can prevent
them, if taken early enough. In a jug combine orange
juice 50/50 with reasonable dry sparkling wine.
  A bottle of sparkling takes ¾ litre orange juice.

CHAPTER 8

The shared environment

The standard of decoration and furnishing in rented accommodation varies enormously, from newly decorated rooms containing antique furniture to peeling walls and furniture that looks as though it has been retrieved from a skip.

What you need in a shared house, and how to make the most of it, depends on the attitudes of the sharers.

The shared parts of the house are usually the sitting room, kitchen and bathroom. You might also have a dining room or a breakfast room and a garden. Obviously the amount of communal space depends upon the size of the house and the relative affluence of its inhabitants. If the house is owner-occupied, it will be better furnished than if it is rented furnished, as few non-resident landlords will put their best furniture out for potential abuse by the tenants. Quite apart from that, most landlords seem to have execrable taste in furniture.

THE SITTING ROOM

The sitting room should have enough space for everyone in the house and one or two more besides to sit comfortably at one time. You may only claim rights to a particular chair if it belongs to you and you are at least ten years older than the mean age of the rest of the household. Otherwise, chairs are taken on a first come, first served basis. As a general rule, modern etiquette allows you to move into someone else's nice chair when they have left the room but not if they have gone out to do everyone a favour like making tea or getting some sandwiches together.

Besides the chairs, the sitting room is the home of the television and other electronic gadgets. Disputes can arise over the choice of entertainment: it should be decided by a majority vote, with the person holding the remote control buttons (or sitting nearest the set) having a casting vote in the event of a tie. If you really find the programme selected unbearable, you are free to leave the room – I find *Dallas* is a good time to do my laundry, while others in our house tend to do their ironing during the Test Match highlights. If the television is rented, it is fair that the rental is shared by the entire household.

A video recorder is probably a worthwhile investment. It is possible to rent video recorders, but I am wary of this since a suspiciously large number of my acquaintances have been burgled shortly after renting a video, and it has always been the video that has been taken. Renting is less economical than buying on credit, if you are creditworthy enough. Once you have a video, you may want to build up a small library of classic films and television programmes. It is a good idea to keep a selection of blank tapes in stock to record films and other programmes: work on the basis of one programme to a tape, which may be wasteful since tapes are quite long but it saves the bother of being sure to have a tape at the right place to start recording. The cost of a new blank tape is relatively minor and prevents the rows that occur when treasured programmes are erased.

Keep your video tapes in three separate categories: Treasures, Recorded and Blank. The Treasures are programmes that are to be kept, and the tapes are marked - perhaps with a sticky label – to identify them as such, and kept in a safe place on a bookshelf. The Recorded and Blank tapes form a pool of tapes for the day-to-day use of the machine; you will probably need half a dozen tapes in the pool. You can keep them in two separate compartments or shoe-boxes next to the video. If you want to record a programme you take a tape from the Blank box, and when it's recorded you put it back in the Recorded box, from which you take it to view. Once you, and anybody else in the house who wants to, has seen the programme and you are all happy not to save it for the future, you put the tape back in the Blank box to be used again. If it turns out to be a Treasure – a really good film, or a fascinating documentary, or the news of a particularly important event, or a classic cricket or rugby match or whatever – you promote it from the pool to the Treasure shelf and buy a new tape to fill in the pool. If only one person considers the programme a Treasure, he or she buys the new blank tape and can even mark the Treasure tape with his or her own name to take on when he or she leaves the house. Strictly speaking, you shouldn't keep the tape for more than 28 days after the programme was first broadcast, even if it is of 'Treasure' status, otherwise you could be sued for breach of copyright. If you were to *sell* such a tape you would be committing the criminal act of piracy.

Usually someone in the house will possess a reasonably good stereo. It is considered more sociable to put it in the sitting room than to keep it in one's own room (unless the sitting room is already thus equipped), but if the equipment is super-delicate this may not be a practical proposition.

However good or bad the equipment, don't bank on your flatmates being careful with records and stereos. People who handle records carelessly, touching the grooves and not putting them back in their sleeves, are not necessarily natural vandals – it may be that they have never been told how to handle records. Use tact and discretion to explain how you would like your precious LPs handled, and most people will happily oblige; if you don't say anything, and your rare mint copy of Prince's *Black* LP is damaged, you have only yourself to blame.

When it comes to choosing which record to play, the choice always lies with the person putting on the record. The same person should turn the record over.

The era of the Walkman has caused previously well organized collections of cassette tapes in shared houses to be ravaged. As you leave the house in the morning (late as usual) you dash into the sitting room looking for a new tape to make the journey bearable and grab the first one that comes to hand. At the same time, you discard the tape that was in your Walkman, and leave it out without its box. By the time five people have done that every day for a week, not a single tape remains in its box and you have 35 tapes with 35 empty boxes. Next Monday, as you set off in the hope of a soothing piece of Chopin to get you to work, you grab the tape you thought was Fou T'Song playing the Nocturnes and end up with Meatloaf or Marillion, which ruins your week. Discipline and order are essential with tapes. Keep the tapes on their own shelf, and when you take one out of its box leave the box in a safe place. When you get back from work, *first* put the tape from your Walkman back in its box then back on the shelf, and *then* take the next tape. Easy, really, isn't it?

The fire
A good sitting room has a fireplace. If you are lucky, it will be an open fire and the house will also have central heating. Getting all your heat from an open fire in winter is no fun, but having a fire is a great comfort, and marvellously convivial on a winter evening. In cities you have to burn smokeless fuel. Smokeless coal takes ages to get going. A fire lit just as you get in from work will be warm and cosy by bedtime. Coal of any description burns with a lot of ash, and the grate needs to be cleaned out (which is a dirty, dusty job) regularly. An alternative is prefabricated reconstituted log-type fuel, some types of which are allowed in smokeless zones. They light quickly and burn quickly, with little ash. However, they are more expensive than coal and give off less heat in the long run (but because they burn more quickly, the fire itself seems hotter). Gas-fired fake fires are getting more convincing, and are much less effort than a real fire; electric fake fires are not at all convincing. With a real fire, you should make sure the chimney is kept swept. Call in a sweep to look at the chimney the first time you use the open fire in a new house, and thereafter have it swept regularly: annually if you have a fire every night in the winter, biennially if you

have one less often. Put a spark guard in front of an open fire if you leave the room, and make sure that at night it's either damped down or banked up.

Keeping the sitting room clean
It is the residue from a relaxed evening which makes a room unpleasant the following morning. Beer is generally more noxious than wine, so try to take beer bottles, cans and glasses out of the sitting room before going to bed. Generally, the more cleaning up you can manage at night the better for all.

If yours is a smoking household, you will probably be immune to the stink of tobacco, but even so for the sake of others it can be reduced. Use ashtrays, and empty them before you go to bed at night. If the household is predominantly non-smoking, try to discourage your guests from smoking – it is a habit which many people find offensive.

Another thing that makes a room smell is food, particularly take-aways in their sodden paper and greasy cartons. If you come home late with a take-away, always try to clear the aftermath away from the sitting room before you go to bed, and try not to spill sweet-and-sour sauce on the carpet.

THE KITCHEN
Our kitchen is ludicrously small. The advantage of this is that no one can argue about the need for communal meals, as there is no way five people could each cook a meal for one in there every night. However, we would prefer a bigger kitchen. A big kitchen, incorporating a breakfast/dining area, makes the household buzz and creates a natural focal point. If this kitchen/dining area can be just off the sitting room, so much the better, because it means that the person doing the cooking is not so isolated from the rest of the house.

The kitting-out of the kitchen is a function of wealth. Modern labour-saving devices usually provide a net benefit. If I had to choose between a new gas cooker and a dishwasher, I'd go for the dishwasher every time provided the old gas cooker still worked. If you have a cooker hood, you will save yourself much cleaning as it helps stop that greasy film of kitchen dust depositing itself everywhere. Extractor hoods are better than filter hoods in this respect. Freezers and microwaves are useful, too; but the one essential item still seen as a luxury in some houses is the washing-machine – which doesn't really belong in a kitchen.

A dishwasher might seem to be a real luxury and an extravagance, but once you've had one, you'll never want to be without. In a shared house, the dishwasher is a real boon. Before we had ours, the kitchen would accumulate dirty tea and coffee mugs, glasses and cereal bowls every day. Even rinsing up your own bowl or mug after use isn't good enough – they never get properly cleaned, and in hard-water areas a brown scum line stays on the mugs. The dishwasher really does make a better job of washing up.

Most modern dishwashers have a 'rinse-only' cycle, which is rather useful. After you've put your bowl and mug in the machine, you run the 'rinse' cycle, which is at least as effective as putting it to soak. Then, when you run the main cycle, with special detergent, the mugs, plates and glasses shine, the cutlery sparkles, and the rows diminish.

Pots, pans, crockery and cutlery are house property by and large; everyone shares them. Mugs and glasses are however perishable: use cheap mugs and glasses (the ones you get with petrol are fine for every day). Quite a few lodgers have bits and pieces of their own, some of which come in handy when added to the general stock of equipment. It's a good idea for everyone in the house to make a list of items which they consider to be specifically theirs and which they would take away on leaving the house. Another idea is to have a little book in the kitchen with a list of whose everything is. However, the risk of lending things to the house has to be borne by the lender. If you lend your Crown Derby plates and they get broken in the washing-up, you can't really blame anyone for it; if you care that much for them, you should wash them up yourself. Some cooks are possessive about their knives or their omelette pans and expect everyone to show the same respect for them as they do. I have known rows develop from this. If you have some special equipment, like knives or pans which need special treatment, you should ask the rest of your flatmates not to use them unless you are happy that they will use them properly. It can, I admit, be very annoying when the seasoning of years on your best crêpe or omelette pan is ruined by an idiot with a scouring pad, but you cannot blame ignorance if you have failed to impart the knowledge.

THE BATHROOM

The bathroom is a bone of contention in most shared flats and houses. We have one golden rule in our house, which is 'Clean the bath', but even that rule doesn't address the main difficulty – the morning queue. In the end you simply must try to time your visits to the bathroom to fit in with everybody else. If you plan a longish bath in the morning, you should either wait until everyone else has used the bathroom or get up early before anyone else needs to use it.

It is important to leave the bathroom and the wash-basin clean; bossy little notices saying 'Please leave the bathroom as you would wish to find it' are both ineffective and unnecessary. Just make sure you rinse the basin and the bath well, and don't leave hair or scum for the next person. It's also a good idea to hang up the bathmat, as it is more likely to dry.

THE GARDEN

The garden is best left as the province of the house's gardener or gardeners, if any. A truly practical communal garden would have no lawn but a collection of attractive, slow-growing shrubs, including lavender, rosemary and bay, which need little or no attention. Unfortunately most gardens have grass, which needs mowing regularly, and flowerbeds, which need weeding. This is fine if one of you actually likes gardening, but in many houses the garden degenerates into a jungle surprisingly quickly. It is worth mowing the grass, at least, for the one or two days in the year when the sun shines.

CLEANING AND HOUSEWORK

The cleaning is, along with the booze cupboard, the telephone and the choice of television viewing, one of the greatest bones of contention in shared houses. If everyone in the house goes out to work, a cleaner is not an extravagance. The difficulty lies in finding a good cleaner; more and more cleaning agencies are being established but all of them have trouble finding experienced cleaners. (Of course, they could train staff, but the cost of this might eat into their margins.) The second difficulty with a cleaner is the security aspect, since you will have to give him or her a key to your house. If you have to be there while the work is done, you might as well do it yourself. You should check, before you give your cleaner a key, that it won't affect your insurance cover.

A cleaner who comes in for two hours twice a week will keep your house under control for less than £20 a week. Compared to the potential for arguments and disputes, this is a negligible sum.

Otherwise, cleaning presents problems. Cleaning rosters are rather too Stalinist; there has to be a better way.

Some people (and I am one of them) are quite tolerant of mess and untidiness; others are much less tolerant. Because everyone likes their living surroundings to be clean and tidy – well, almost everyone – the people with the lowest mess tolerance always end up doing more cleaning and tidying. Tidiness is a virtue in a shared house, and the tidier and cleaner you are the better a lodger you will be. If you are a natural slob, you should try to make a bit more of an effort, particularly when you are being nagged about it. On the other hand, a house with four or five people living in it will inevitably be more untidy than a flat with only one or two inhabitants (this can be mathematically proven: it has something to do with entropy) and it will be better for your own well-being, and for the general atmosphere, if you can avoid getting too uptight about tidiness. The best flatmates are naturally tidy, but they don't mind untidiness and are relaxed about other people's mess: this is a rare combination of virtues.

One way round the problem is to set aside a weekly cleaning time, when everyone does some cleaning if present. Cleaning time is slightly reminiscent of 'happy hour', an important part of the daily routine on board many ships when the crew gets down to cleaning and scrubbing. Be wary of skivers who decide that they have an urgent appointment with a football at this moment.

Another way of persuading your flatmates that it's time some cleaning was done is to fuss around, cleaning up, and then go and get the hoover out just as *Dallas* or the football is starting. This works fairly well with women and New Men, but old-style men are quite impervious to the hint being hopefully dropped by someone rushing around with a duster, and a hoover will just make them feel more at home.

Another method is to allocate specific areas of the house as the particular responsibility of one person. If you know that the fridge is rancid but it's so-and-so's job to keep the fridge clean and tidy, you are quite entitled to nag him. The advantages of this system are that each person can be responsible for the bits that he or she feels most strongly about, uses most or notices most. (My parents used to share the cleaning in their house, which they did before breakfast. They would take it in turns to cook breakfast, and the other would do some housework. My mother would always notice if the floors were dirty, and was always hoovering and sweeping, while my father never noticed the floor but liked things to be dusted, so he always did the dusting.)

If you feel you are doing more than your fair share of tidying and cleaning, don't bottle it up and worry about it. For a start, most of the other slobs in the house probably haven't even noticed, so you must bring it to their attention. When you do bring it to their attention, you must try not to criticize, because it will put them on the defensive. Your aim is not to cause a row but to get the slobs to do some cleaning and tidying. Choose your moment carefully, and play it like this:

'By the way, guys, don't you think the place is a bit of a tip? Shouldn't we do some cleaning?'

They will reply, 'Yes – I suppose it could do with a quick once-over with a hoover' or some such, and 'When are you going to do it?' (being provocative).

You *might* then say, 'Me! Why is it always *me* that has to do the b***** cleaning? Why don't some of you lazy b******* do some cleaning for a change? I'm fed up with waiting on you hand and foot' and storm off to your room in tears.

This may have some short-term effects – they might for example rinse their tea mugs before going to the pub – but the better answer is, 'Well, it needs doing *now*. How about it?'

They will reply: 'Well, we're just off out now . . .'

You: 'Of course. The trouble is, I've got to go out as well. But if you guys all muck in we'll have it done in no time . . .'

Regardless of whether or not you have a cleaner, the house will be easier to clean if everyone observes some basic courtesies, such as rinsing the bath, putting cereal bowls to soak and washing the occasional glass or mug.

To sum up, if you want to keep the house clean, there are three basic ways of achieving this, and they are not mutually exclusive:

(1) get a cleaner;
(2) do some cleaning yourself;
(3) don't get mad if the others don't do their fair share – get even.

INDIVIDUAL ROOMS:
SUGGESTIONS FOR LANDLORDS

What goes on behind the closed door of a lodger's room is his/her business, within reason. What is reasonable for the lodger depends to some extent upon what kind of a room you, as the landlord, have provided: the line between acceptable and unacceptable is what causes serious damage (beyond wear and tear) to your property. However, if you have a cleaner who does individual rooms, that will be a good incentive for lodgers to keep their floors clear of unwashed smalls.

If you are charging a stiff rent, you should provide a decent room. Your lodger may decide to turn down a room that looks like one of the ones the Salvation Army decided not to let, but so often any room is better than the streets or the friend's living-room floor. Because the lodger is in such a disadvantaged position, the only incentive to you, the landlord, to provide a good room is a moral one – plus the fact that it makes the whole household more civilized.

The only opportunity you will have to decorate the lodger's room is at change-of-lodger time, so that's a good reason to consider redecorating, perhaps over a weekend, between one going and another arriving. However, there's no point in going over the top with expensive wallpaper and flashy paint jobs. Most people like to put their own pictures and posters up in their own rooms, to impose a little of their own identity on the place. You shouldn't therefore mind if your lodger uses bluetack or picture hooks. If there's a reason why you want him or her to be very careful with the walls, then you should help him or her hang pictures, providing proper hooks and so on yourself.

Bedrooms should have fitted carpets made from wool or wool-mixture. All-synthetic is nasty, especially to walk on barefoot. A small rug next to the bed makes the room look more welcoming and is not an expensive addition. It should be made entirely from natural fibres. The bed you provide must be in good condition, not sagging. Don't fob your lodgers off with a bed you would never sleep in yourself; you could cripple them. Most people find a medium-to-firm bed comfortable enough. For a single bed, the standard size is now 3 feet 6 inches wide, although there are still a lot of 3-foot beds around. Try to provide 3-foot 6-inch beds. The bed should have a headboard; not only does this make the bed more comfortable, it also protects your walls from being marked by hair. Most (but not all) people nowadays have their own duvet, sheets, duvet covers and pillow-cases, so the only bedding you should have to provide is an underblanket and pillows. If you do provide a duvet, provide a synthetic one: not only will it be cheaper than a down one but it can be used by asthmatics, who are often allergic to the feathers in natural duvets; also, it can be washed in a machine. Down duvets must of course be dry-cleaned by specialist cleaners. Put plain under-pillow-cases on the pillows and they will last longer.

You must provide a wardrobe or other hanging space for a dozen or so outfits. However much space you provide, it is unlikely to be enough. A chest-of-drawers, or, failing a chest-of-drawers, a cupboard with easily accessible open shelves, for storing loose items of clothing and underwear, is essential. The top of the chest-of-drawers may double for a dressing-table: your lodger will need a looking-glass and space for potions, powders, paints and pomades. A bedside table with a bedside light should not be too far from a socket outlet, with room for a radio/alarm and a glass of water. A desk or writing table and chair are also necessary; your lodger may well be studying for professional exams, or may need to bring work home. A bookcase and a waste-paper basket should be provided too.

For taking the chill off a room quickly in cold weather an electric heater (preferably a fan heater) is important, and more economical than heating the entire house. If the house is centrally heated, the bedroom radiators should be fitted with thermostatic valves.

DEALING WITH LAUNDRY

The ideal arrangement is to keep the washing-machine in a separate room, together with several drying-racks and an ironing-board. This will cut out the need for visits to the laundrette, and enable you to dry clothes out of other public areas.

Not all houses are so well equipped. Most kitchen designers seem to think that washing-machines belong in the kitchen. This is a typically male attitude, based on the assumption that all domestic work comes into the same category, so that the kitchen becomes the Woman's Room – or, more to the point, the Housewife's Room. Preparing food and washing linen have very little in common, in fact, and benefit from being kept well apart. However, if you do have to have your washing-machine in the kitchen, then you need enough space for it. Drying of clothes really *must* be done elsewhere, otherwise your clean laundry will pick up the smells of cooking onions and hot fat.

The advice that follows is for those people, usually men, who have been brought up in an environment where the passage of clothes from laundry basket or bedroom floor back to the sock drawer is a mystery at least as unfathomable as the nature of women's underclothing and considerably less interesting.

As you will no doubt discover for yourself, clothes do not get clean and pressed of their own accord. The reason they appear to have done so up to now is that your poor mother has been doing it for you. You are now on your own, and laundry will be an ongoing problem. One solution is to send it to a laundry, but that is expensive.

Washing-machines

If you are at all lucky your flatshare will have an automatic washing-machine. If the washing-machine is not an automatic you will find it easier to take your clothes to the laundrette.

Automatic washing-machines are usually plumbed in, and have a door at the front, a selection of control knobs and buttons, a filter and a soap compartment. You put your clothes in, shut the door, put your washing powder in the compartment, set the controls and switch it on. The machine will go through its washing cycle, which can take up to five hours, finishing with a long spin when it makes a hell of a racket and shakes itself almost to pieces. Some women like to sit on washing-machines. Your clothes end up in a wet crumpled mass and have to be hung out to dry or put in a dryer, unless the machine incorporates a drier.

The complicated part of working a washing-machine is deciphering the control knobs and buttons. By way of differentiating their products, each washing-machine manufacturer makes his control knobs and buttons work differently from anyone else's. On the whole, washing-machines tend to have two main programmes – a normal and a delicate wash. The normal wash will probably be available with or without a pre-wash, and the pre-wash is sometimes extended to a bio pre-wash, or bio cycle. These programmes are controlled in most machines by a knob which rotates as the cycle progresses. You turn the knob to the start of the cycle you want, press the 'go' button, and the machine begins, continues to the end of the cycle, then stops. The other aspect you need to control is the wash temperature. Hot water is a better solvent than warm or cold water, so it shifts muck better. Unfortunately, very hot water has other less desirable effects. Being a better solvent of muck also makes it a better solvent of dye, so colours can run if the water is too hot. Hot water melts plastic, and synthetic fibres, made out of long thin bits of plastic, can become mis-shapen, while wool and silk can be shrunk by hot water. Only white cotton and linen are immune to really hot water, and it is rare to have a full load of items in these fabrics nowadays.

Most washing-machines have a separate temperature control, either a row of buttons or a knob, displaying temperatures of 95°C, 60°C and 40°C.

Washing-machines come with a host of other gizmos, which vary from machine to machine:

(1)   a wool cycle, which limits the rinse temperature so that woollen items are less likely to shrink;
(2)   a short spin button, which spins the clothes for half the usual time, which is better for jerseys and other woollen items;
(3)   an economy button, which uses less water for small loads;
(4)   a spin-only button, which allows you to spin-dry hand-washed items.

Laundrettes

Laundrettes are fitted with heavy-duty machines which have a much more limited range of programmes than domestic ones but which are still entirely adequate for most purposes. If you have any choice of programme at all, it is usually either Normal or Delicate (hot or warm). The machines are much quicker than home machines, because they don't have to heat the water – it comes from the laundrette's main steam boiler. A wash takes about half an hour. The laundrette may have big spin-dryers and will have a bank of tumble-dryers. The spin-dryer, or extractor, will get a lot of water out of the washed items, so you should put them in the spin-dryer before putting them in the tumble-dryer. Laundrette tumble-dryers have a voracious appetite for coin of the realm.

Hand-washing

Some things are best hand-washed, and sometimes hand-washing is the only option open to you – for example, when the washing-machine has broken down, the laundrette is shut and you need some clean clothes for tomorrow. Wash delicate clothes just by swishing them about in washing solution; mucky clothes and cottons need to be scrubbed. By and large, you should only ever need to wash delicate clothes by hand. Boiling whites (but only those made of natural fibres) which have previously been soaked is a good way of cleaning them: use a huge saucepan on the gas stove.

Powders and potions

There is an enormous variety of washing powders, soap powders, soaking powders and fabric-conditioning liquids. Washing powders can be soap- or detergent-based; biological or non-biological; and automatic or non-automatic; and to add to the confusion, most are now available in liquid form as well. Soap powders are the oldest type and are fairly gentle in their action. Detergents are stronger and better cleaners than soaps (but some types claim to be gentle). Soap powders and flakes are good for hand-washing. The liquids are more concentrated than the powders.

Biological powders contain an enzyme which loosens some types of dirt; the enzyme only works at medium and low temperatures. If you wash with a biological powder at a hot temperature it behaves like an ordinary detergent powder. The way to get the best out of biological powders is first to soak your laundry in a warm solution and then to wash in a hot solution. You could use an ordinary powder for the second stage.

Automatic powders are nothing of the sort. They are for automatic washing-machines (that is, all modern washing-machines) and don't froth up like non-automatic powders. Too much froth in a washing-machine clogs up its works. You *must* therefore use an automatic powder in your washing-machine; you can hand-wash with an automatic powder but you won't get any suds. The suds in non-automatic detergent powders are in any case purely cosmetic.

Biological pre-soakers, which are effective but expensive, contain more of the enzyme and less of the detergent than biological washing-powders contain. You'll get good results if you use one of these for soaking and the pre-wash and an ordinary automatic detergent powder for the second wash.

Stain-looseners are strong detergents which you put over particularly grubby marks before the wash. Those sold in aerosol form are less good value.

The main benefit of fabric conditioners is that they scent the washing. You add them to the wash at the final rinse stage. Fabric conditioners also soften the water, which enables the detergent to be rinsed away more effectively in hard water areas.

Washing shirts
These are the biggest problem area for home washing, which is why many cleaners offer a shirt service for about £1 a go. Your shirts will probably be cotton or polyester-cotton mix. Cotton shirts are slightly more expensive and rather more comfortable than polyester-cotton.

White cotton shirts

Home washing-machine with bio cycle Use the bio cycle, including a pre-wash, and maximum temperature. Put the pre-soaking agent into the pre-wash soap compartment and a good (automatic) detergent into the other compartment.

Home washing-machine without bio cycle Soak your shirts overnight in a bucket with a cupful of pre-soaking agent and warm water. Next day wash on the maximum programme at maximum temperature, with good detergent in the soap compartment. You can also spray the collars and cuffs with a stain-loosener. If you do this you won't need to soak your shirts.

Laundrette Spray your collars and cuffs with stain-loosener before washing, and use the hottest, most vigorous programme possible on the machine.

Coloured cotton shirts and polyester-cotton shirts Follow the same procedure, but make sure the temperature is below maximum. Don't mix coloured and white items of clothing, and always wash a new coloured garment several times on its own before washing it with other things.

Drying shirts

At home, as soon as your shirts come out of the machine hang them to dry on hangers. This will greatly reduce the ironing effort. For polyester-cotton, fill a sink with the hottest water you can bear, and put in your polyester-cotton shirts. Take them out and put them on hangers without wringing, and let them drip dry. You will find they then need little or no ironing.

At the laundrette, put them in the spinner and then the tumble-dryer. Fold them while they're still hot, and whatever you do don't crumple them. Polyester-cotton shirts will need very little ironing if you do this.

Ironing shirts

Cotton shirts will need to be ironed. Traditionally, cotton shirts are ironed while still slightly damp, which leaves them beautifully crisp and shiny. This is a bit of a drag, because you have to wait until they're at exactly the right dryness, then iron the lot. Ironing one shirt is boring enough, but ironing a dozen is stupefying. Thankfully, the electric steam iron means that you can allow your cotton shirts to get completely dry and iron them as you need them, perhaps in the morning before getting dressed for work. You need a steam iron and you should use it pretty hot.

First of all, check the bottom of the iron. This is important, because if one of your flatmates has ironed a plastic garment at the wrong temperature you will find half the Nottinghamshire coalfield stuck to the bottom of the iron. If this is the case, use a green scouring pad dipped in cold water to remove it.

Now check that there's enough water in the iron. Turn it on, and set the temperature knob to the correct setting for cotton.

Start ironing your shirt at the inside of the cuffs. This bit doesn't show, so if there is any muck on the iron, or your shirt is actually poly-cotton and the iron is therefore too hot, no real harm will be done. Iron the inside of the cuff, then the outside, then lay the sleeve out flat so that one of the folds passes along the seam of the sleeve. Iron well, then turn the sleeve over to iron the other side. Do the same with the other arm.

Now put the shirt over the end of the ironing-board, so that the board tip appears to be going down one arm-hole. Iron the shoulders and the neck – the part of the shirt known as the yoke, and then move it to do the other side. Now iron the button flap, first from behind to make it lie flat, and then from the front, ironing between the buttons, and do the same with the button-hole flap. Lay the shirt on the ironing-board with the collar over the end of the board and the front tail on the button side out flat. Iron carefully, then rotate the shirt so that you are doing the back, and go round again until you have the button-hole side of the shirt in front of you. Iron this, and you have only the collar to do.

Iron the collar by folding it out flat and ironing first the inside of the collar, on the outside of the shirt, and finally the bit that shows, the outside of the collar.

If you are not going to wear the shirt immediately, put it on a hanger. If you are packing a suitcase, fold the shirt. To do this, first do up the buttons. Lay the shirt front-downwards on the ironing-board; make the first fold from the shoulder to the tail down one side, then fold back the sleeve. Do the same from the other side, then fold up the tail.

Polyester-cotton shirts are ironed in exactly the same way, except that the iron *must not be too hot*. It should be set just below two dots. If it is too hot, the shirt will first wrinkle, then burn, leaving muck on the iron.

Washing socks and underclothes
These are best washed on a normal cycle at medium-hot temperature, about 60°C. Hang out to dry, or spin first then tumble-dry.

Washing jeans
Once you have done your shrink-to-fit bit with your 501s, they shouldn't shrink any more and being cotton are resistant to fairly intensive washing. The colour in denim is very runny, so you should apply a strict colour bar until you have got well-faded jeans. Cotton corduroy trousers wash in the same way.

Washing cotton jersey
This encompasses sweat-shirts, T-shirts and track-suits, which should be washed in the machine as for coloured cotton. However, the stretchy jersey material needs to be treated a bit more carefully at the drying stage. If the spin-drying was effective, you should be able to hang the garments on hangers and just pull them into shape, but if the washing-machine is a little geriatric it won't spin brilliantly. To preserve the shape of these garments, let them dry flat for a bit.

Washing woollens
Woven wool, such as tweed, worsted and flannel, should be dry-cleaned. Jumpers can be washed, either by hand

or using the wool cycle of a domestic washing-machine. Don't wash jumpers in a laundrette machine.

To wash woollens by hand, first run a bowlful of hand-hot water and add soap powder, or Lux flakes, or Dreft, or Stergene or Woolite. Swish it around, then add your woollens and swish them around for a few minutes. If you have a separate spin-dryer or a washing-machine which can easily be used as a spin-dryer (by moving the dial to just before the end of the main wash cycle), put the woollens in and spin for a few seconds. Empty your washing-bowl, fill it with warm water, then rinse the woollens. Spin them dry for a few seconds between rinses if possible: this will reduce the total number of rinses you need. You should rinse the items at least three times, with fresh warm water for each rinse. If you cannot spin between rinses, you will need at least five rinses. You will get a better rinse if you have soft water (in London, for example, the water is hard: to make it soft, if you don't have a water-softener plumbed in, you can add a softening agent to the water).

Finally, give the woollens a final spin lasting about 40 seconds. If you can't spin them, lay your woollens over the bath on a flat rack to drip dry. If they hang vertically while full of water, the weight of water will pull them out of shape.

Once they're damp-dry, having been spun, the woollens should still be dried flat. The easiest way to do this is to spread a clean bath-towel on the floor and leave them, laid out flat and pulled into shape, to dry there.

Washing towels and bed-linen
None of these present any great difficulty beyond their unwieldiness. It's a good idea to do up the studs on the open edge of a duvet cover before putting it in the machine, to stop the rest of the washing ending up inside it. Towels take ages and ages to dry; if you can't hang them outside in the sun put them over a radiator.

DRY-CLEANING
Suits and similar heavy items of clothing have to be

dry-cleaned. This is a simple operation which involves taking the clothes to the dry-cleaners, having first made sure that the pockets are empty and after removing any belts or buckles. When you hand the clothes in you'll be given a ticket in exchange. The next day, or whenever you are told the items will be ready, you take back your ticket, pay the ransom and collect your clothes.

Ties also have to be dry-cleaned. Ties are unbelievably complicated to clean, and no dry-cleaner can do them properly in less than about a week. They will cost you nearly as much as a suit to have cleaned.

The law of lunch/tie attraction
This law states that lunch is attracted to ties, and it goes on to say that the more attractive the tie, the more lunch is attracted to it. A new, very smart and distinctive silk tie will proceed to promiscuous intimacy with lunch seconds into their first meeting. The same tie will be just as rampant with lunch just after a visit to the cleaners. Lunch is much less attracted to dull, uninspiring ties, and if you are concerned about your tie-cleaning budget you should wear only sombre polyester ties.

CLEANING
Again, much of the advice in this section is for the newcomer (probably male) to household chores, particularly if he is the type who regards the hoover as the fearsome monster that makes a lot of unnecessary noise during the cricket.

Dusting should be done before vacuuming, however, because it raises dust. Swishing around with a feather duster is not enough; you have to lift up all the junk and ornaments on the shelves and other surfaces you are dusting. Use a soft yellow duster. It is a good idea to spray-polish wooden surfaces, because this means that the duster absorbs the dust instead of simply pushing it on to the floor, or wherever. Valuable furniture should be polished with an old-fashioned furniture cream or with pure beeswax; other wooden surfaces can be polished with a beeswax spray. Polishes which come in aerosol cans are expensive and damage the ozone layer, but fortunately good polishes in trigger sprays are now available.

The vacuum cleaner has an invaluable role to play in keeping the floors of your flat or house clean. Vacuum cleaners come in two types, the upright and the floor model; the upright is less versatile but it combines the sucking action with a brushing action and does a better job on most types of carpet. With floor models, it is important to use the correct head on the end of the hose: you use the head without brushes or with brushes retracted; with the brushes extended, you can vacuum hard surfaces; you will also find other attachments, the most useful of which is a narrow nozzle that enables you to clean in corners, under furniture and right to the edge of fitted carpets.

Vacuum cleaners give up if they are not emptied regularly; and the hoses can get blocked if you try to suck up bits that are too big. To unblock a hose, a good method is to reconnect it so that the machine is blowing rather than sucking: on most cylinder machines, this means connecting it to the opposite end of the cylinder. Point the end of the hose at the hole on the machine that does the sucking and switch on.

To do an effective job with the vacuum cleaner, you should first of all tidy the room, removing books, papers and so on from the floor and chairs. Then concentrate on the bits under the chairs and in the corners; they are so much more difficult to do that if you concentrate on them you will find the open spaces in the centre of the room almost do themselves.

From time to time windows need to be cleaned. Cleaning windows is easy with a rubber squeegee; expensive window-cleaning fluids are usually unnecessary. Use the squeegee, soapy water and a chamois leather to finish off.

Washing-up is the biggest bore of all. For this reason, you are well advised to persuade your flatmates to invest in a dishwasher. Even so, there will still be items to wash up on occasion. To do this, use very hot water, and wear rubber gloves. If you can bear the water

Flatshare, Houseshare

without gloves, it's not hot enough. If you have a double sink, fill one with hot soapy water and the other with hot clean water. Start with the glasses and fill the soapy sink with glasses. Carefully remove the glasses from the soapy sink and clean off any dried-on lines or lipstick marks with a cloth or your fingers. Then rinse the glasses in the rinse sink and leave to drain. If the water was hot enough, they will drain dry quite quickly but with hard water they will be streaky, so you should dry them up. (Before you do this, fill the wash sink with mugs and cups.) Use a clean linen or linen union tea-towel and dry them while they are still hot. When the tea-towel is wet, put it to one side and get another one out of the drawer – damp tea-towels harbour germs and they should really only be used once before being washed again. Not drying up at all is in fact much more hygienic.

Wash the mugs or cups next, paying particular attention to the brown scum line.

Leave the mugs in the rinse sink while you fill the wash sink with the next batch which can soak while you empty the rinse sink, and so on until the washing up is finished.

Washing up with a single sink is less satisfactory. It is customary in many households not to rinse off the suds but to dry them off with a tea-towel. This is doubly ineffectual, because the tea-towel spreads germs and leaves the soapy taste on the dishes. The best solution is to leave the tap running slowly while you wash up and rinse the items under it before leaving them to drain.

CHAPTER 9

Parties

From time to time you will probably want to give a party. Don't give them too often, or you'll get stale, but when you *do* give one make sure that it's one to remember. Nothing is worse than a bad shared-house party, with poor organization, not enough room to move and both loos out of action owing to their occupation by comatose drunks. A good, well-planned party on the other hand, is an excellent way of making a house-share come alive.

Parties come in various shapes and sizes, from the quiet dinner party to the mega-thrash. In most flats and houses, the limitations of space and neighbours preclude the mega-thrash, which really needs be held in a big megabuck country house. The largest party you can probably accommodate will be something in the order of a demi-mega-thrash.

A demi-mega-thrash is hard work for all involved. Major furniture removals will be required and decorations will take time, ingenuity and money.

Drinks parties, dinner parties and the like are simpler to organize and just as much fun, if not quite so memorable. You can give dinner parties weekly, have a drinks party at Christmas, a buffet lunch for your birthday, and a demi-mega-thrash every two or three years.

THE DEMI-MEGA-THRASH
Here I can do no better than describe the best such party in which I have ever been involved. It was given

by some friends of mine, in a shared house I had since left. However, I was a fairly regular visitor there, and along with everybody else around I became caught up in the enthusiasm and the preparation. Like many such parties, this one had a theme, which in this case was *Thriller*: Michael Jackson's LP and video had just been released and were in the charts as well as being constantly broadcast on the airwaves.

Notification to guests was by way of invitation – a little plastic bag containing what looked as though they might be entrails. The bag was sealed with a folded cardboard label, with the words 'Thriller Bag' printed in large, ghoulish letters in black and red, with details of the address and time in small letters below. The 'entrails' had been made by boiling pasta shapes with food colouring and adding a bilious greenish mixture of flour and water. (Unfortunately, no preservative had been added. The invitations were sent by mail and arrived on people's doormats in June and July, when many were away on holiday. The hot weather caused the contents to ferment, and a number of these bags exploded, giving the recipients rather more of a thrill than intended.)

Although not specifically stated on the invitation, it was clear that fancy dress was expected. When asked, guests were told to come as Michael Jackson or something from a horror movie. All the guests made a real effort with the fancy dress, and some extraordinarily bizarre costumes appeared.

The front door of the house had been specially decorated. A huge pair of papier-mâché lips surrounded the entire porch, with fangs protruding. Guests had to enter through this mouth. The hallway had been draped with blankets dyed dark grey, forming a black tunnel, the 'throat', through which everyone had to walk before reaching the party. Inside the throat dangled various unpleasant surprises, such as furry spiders and soft, rubbery hands – made by filling surgical gloves with a soft cornflour paste. From there the passageway led to a darkened kitchen, by way of a cardboard skeleton which would jump out at you, bathed in dazzling light, every now and again. To the right was the dance room, the through lounge of the house, which also led into the kitchen. The dance room was lit only by ultra-violet light and the eerie glow from two giant television monitors playing *The Creature from the Black Lagoon*. The dark faces of dancers were highlighted by flashes of light from the spots of day-glo colour on their clothing and their bodies. The kitchen was a passageway, although the cookers contained food – in the form of french bread pizzas – which were dished out later as people got hungry. At the end of the kitchen were french windows, leading out into the garden. The frame of the french windows had been transformed into a guillotine, and the blade, fortunately made only of hardboard, would come crashing down from time to time.

In the garden was an altar where there were signs of human sacrifices having recently been performed – the heads and hands from tailors' dummies were used to suggest this. In front of the altar was a coffin, in which – besides a clearly decomposed 'body' – lay a hundredweight of ice, and chilling bottles of sparkling wine. The ground was covered with drifting fog and smoke – from a hired special-effect smoke generator – while from the mist the arm of a monstrous octopus flailed after anything that seemed to move.

Beyond the coffin and the altar lay further gravestones. The graves were those of the hosts, with a suitable epitaph for each one: polystyrene had been painted grey to make the stones, and a load of granite chips had been spread out to mark out the grave plots. Various limbs appeared not to have been properly buried. The tree at the end of the garden had recently been pressed into service as a lynch-pole, for a body was still hanging from the noose. Nearby a fire burned, with a cauldron full of rats, mice and human appendages merrily bubbling over the flames.

That was just the decoration. The music was good, loud and designed for dancing, and everyone had come with the intention and the expectation of a good time. The work of putting the decorations in place had created a spirit of excitement amongst the hosts, their close friends and house-guests, who had spent the best part of the previous month preparing for it. For those less closely involved, it was the time spent preparing costumes that built up the excitement.

Everybody wanted to come to the party, and so bizarre were the costumes that few people went to a pub or bar beforehand. By 9.30 in the evening, almost everyone had arrived, and the party continued until six or so the next day. There were no drunken gate-crashers looking for a piss-up; and although everyone drank enough, few people overdid it.

Such thrashes don't have to be at night. Sunday lunch-time is quite a good time to have a thrash, and one year I did that. We wrote out invitations to a buffet lunch as simple, hand-written 'at homes'. However, we arranged for a jazz trio to be playing and erected a canopy in the garden. The kitchen table was the buffet table, with a fairly exotic spread of salads and meats. We made up a lethal cocktail of sparkling wine, peach wine and vodka, with chopped peaches as a garnish, and dispensed it in jugs. Few people were expecting quite so many guests – we had asked a hundred – and the alcohol quickly loosened people's tongues. Our last guests left, long after the jazz musicians had packed up and gone, at one the next morning (the party had started a mere twelve hours earlier). Natural body-clocks were less put out than they might have been with an all-night thrash, and yet afterwards there were just as many recriminations and blushes.

Getting the theme, or style, of a party right is important. Fancy dress is an excellent way of getting people in the right mood. After that, it's just a matter of getting the other details right. Good drink, good food and good music are the essentials. Punches and cocktails are a good idea, but make sure you decide on the recipe and ask your guests to bring the right ingredients. It's quite acceptable to put a style of drink after the PBAB on the invitation – the normal requests are white or sparkling wine. If you're asking people to bring spirits, don't expect more than a half-bottle between two, but generally spirits should not be expected.

Scotland has a different drink tradition: that of BYOB, or Bring Your Own Bevy. In Scotland, the world divides into whisky-drinkers and vodka-drinkers, and everyone brings their own drink to a party, which they hang on to throughout, perhaps offering friends a dram from their own bottle. This is the way in which Scots celebrate the best party of all, the bacchanal of Hogmanay. At other times, the Scots tradition leaves parties with hundreds of little piles of carry-out bags, tripping up dancers and giving necking couples nasty bruises. When giving parties in Scotland, I have found it quite acceptable – if a little unusual – to ask guests to donate their carry-outs to a central drink station, as in England, although this means limiting the choice to whisky, vodka, Export or Sharons'n'Karens.

Most of your guests will have come to the party with the intention of having a drink or two, but one or two heroes may have volunteered to drive people home. You should provide some kind of non-alcoholic drink for those who don't want to drink, bearing in mind that Coke might be O.K. for 10-year-olds but is a bit sweet and cloying for grown-ups, particularly after the fifth. Fruit juices mixed with fizzy mineral water are a good starting point for non-alcoholic drinks. Low-alcohol lager (at the moment the most highly regarded are Klausthaler, Swan Light and Tennents LA) is also very acceptable to those who like lager, but the low-alcohol wines are generally a bit of a failure.

DINNER PARTIES

At a dinner party, you will want everyone to sit down at table, and you will engage in conversation. Because it's unlikely that your dining table will seat many more people than the total number of residents, it's a good idea to have a house rule about disinvitations.

A disinvitation is a message saying, 'I am having a party on — [date] and I would be grateful if you do not come'. Between co-domesticates, the disinvitation is not an insult but a practicality. If you get a disinvitation, go to the pictures and get a take-away. You don't have to stay away until all your co-domesticate's guests have left; but you should not really be in the house. It makes life very uncomfortable for guests if there is the lurking presence of an uninvited and unwanted person in another room.

One good arrangement is to have a general, assumed disinvitation for all dinner parties, so that if you want your co-domesticates to come to one of your dinner parties you have to invite them specifically. However, you must make sure that you give adequate notice of your dinner party to those you will be disinviting, whether that disinvitation is particular or general.

Equality of numbers

When we were young and courting, it seemed very important to have an equal number of men and women at dinner parties, arranged neatly boy-girl, boy-girl round the table, with no partners sitting next to each other. This is extremely heterosexist, and now that we are grown-up and a bit more settled, we're not concerned with pairing our guests off. Instead, we try to invite each guest as an individual in his or her own right, regardless of gender. On the other hand, the form is generally that one should ask both parts of an established couple. Personally I feel that you should only ask both parts of an established couple – married or not – if you happen to know both of them. No one should be asked merely as an appendage of someone else. However, once you have got the couple inside, split them up. It is far better for couples not to sit next to each other; after all, they see each other every day of the week and this is an opportunity for you to give each of them the chance to talk to someone new.

If you are going to have equal sexes, and you want to be very traditional and have the hostess at one end of the table with the host at the other, the male guest of honour sitting to the right of the hostess and the female guest of honour sitting to the right of the host, then be warned that the seating plan will only work if you have an odd number of couples in total, or an even number of lady guests. It won't work with a single lady guest, or two couples; six people – three couples, two lady guests – is ideal, but eight won't work while ten will. In all other respects eight is perhaps the ideal number of people to have at a dinner table.

The primary purpose of a dinner party is not food but conversation. Food, however, comes a close second, because your guests won't enjoy themselves if the food is yucky.

There's no need to turn dinner parties into a culinary competition, however. Know your limits as far as cooking is concerned, and bear in mind that even if you're the best cook in the world you will have time constraints if you hold your party during the week. If you've got to spend the whole time in the kitchen instead of chatting to your guests the occasion will not be much fun either for you or for them.

This menu that follows can be prepared quickly and easily and needs little cooking.

With drinks	*Garlicky olives*
Hors d'oeuvres	*Mackerel pâté*
	Hot french bread
Main course	*Spicy chicken*
	Fresh pasta with olive oil and parmesan
	Salad
Pudding	*Chocolate roulade*
	Cheese
	Fruit

Shopping guide
Garlicky olives and freshly grated parmesan cheese come from the local Italian delicatessen.

Pâté can be bought from the delicatessen or from a supermarket delicatessen counter. For the french bread buy part-baked sticks and re-heat in an oven.

Spicy chicken is a Marks & Spencer ready-meal. Fresh pasta is widely available and can be cooked in 5 minutes. When it's done, toss it in a bowl with olive oil, black pepper and parmesan cheese, and serve immediately.

Ready-prepared salad comes from the better supermarkets, or Marks & Spencer, but it's cheaper, and nearly as easy, to buy a good lettuce (in summer) or Chinese leaves (in winter), wash it and add interesting bits and pieces – for example, satsuma segments, diced Cox's apples, walnuts, black olives, diced farmhouse Cheddar cheese, Belgian chicory, pickled walnuts, cherry tomatoes, celery, sweet pepper, grated carrot, or beansprouts.

Chocolate roulade can also be bought from M & S. Alternatively you could buy an attractive-looking gâteau from a good patisserie.

Cheese is available from your local cheese shop or a good supermarket cheese counter. Fresh fruit can be bought in the market, or even from a supermarket if you are prepared to pay higher prices. Include a ripe mango or a pineapple in your fruit bowl for a touch of luxury.

This is the kind of meal of which no one need be ashamed, especially if you are serving it on a weekday evening, despite the fact that you won't have spent hours preparing it and you won't have a mountain of dishes to wash afterwards. But if you want to display your culinary skills, make Saturday your entertaining day and spend all day in the kitchen.

I like to provide all the drink for a dinner party myself. This way I can select a wine to accompany the meal which will set it off well. The form, however, is for guests to take a bottle of wine. Don't feel that you should have to serve the wine your guests have brought that evening – they will be quite happy to drink yours, provided it really does complement the meal. You can keep the bottle your guests brought for another occasion.

Sherry or gin and tonic are both acceptable pre-prandial drinks, while port is splendid afterwards (although disastrous for drivers and guaranteed to cause a hangover). While alcohol will loosen the inhibitions and may improve the flow of conversation, don't forget that some of your guests may be driving home and others may not be drinking alcohol for health or religious reasons. Provide some interesting non-alcoholic drinks: one of the most palatable is cloudy English apple juice diluted 50-50 with fizzy mineral water.

The end of a dinner party means washing-up. We have a rough rule of thumb about guests washing up: on their first visit to a house they mustn't; on their second they may; and on their third they must. If people are a bit drunk, no one washes up and the work is left until the following day. If this happens, one's co-domesticates are faced with the unappetizing aftermath at breakfast the next day. A compromise, if you really can't face washing up (the only legitimate excuse besides inebriation is that there is no hot water), is to tidy up by piling the plates neatly and leave the cutlery to soak in a pan of cold water; emptying all the glasses and rinsing them in cold water; putting saucepans to soak; and wiping down the worktops. Make sure that the sink is empty and give it a wipe. If you do this after the meal you will find that the washing-up will take hardly any time when you tackle it the next day, with lots of hot water.

DRINKS PARTIES

The 'drinks' is in my (humble) opinion a diabolical invention. It is stupendously popular amongst Sloanes, yuppies, aspirant Sloanes and the like during December, when all kinds of people who haven't seen each other for years hold chi-chi 'drinks'. A 'drinks' is held, competitively, on a weekday after work, and everyone arrives in suits and ties, swallows the glass of wine handed to them and starts braying while munching on a crudité dunked in cottage-cheese dip.

Perhaps I am being a little harsh. It may be that what is wrong with 'drinks' is the people who go to the ones to which I am invited. However, it always seems to me that the dullest part of any party is the standing around chatting while the guests get drunk enough to want to dance (the dancing being the best bit). At a 'drinks' this dull part becomes the sole reason for the party.

If you must have a drinks party, follow some simple rules:

(1)   invite interesting people, without allowing one pro-
      fession to dominate.
(2)   provide a good, strong drink for people as they arrive
      and try to stop people bringing their cars; in cold
      weather the best drink is undoubtedly the champagne
      cocktail, which need not contain champagne but
      should contain, in addition to cheap fizz, angostura
      bitters, a measure of brandy, and a sugar lump (add
      the fizz last); later on you can cut out the brandy.
(3)   try to offer something a little more original than
      crudités on the snack front (apart from anything
      else, crudités with cottage-cheese dip generate scum
      on the surface of one's drink).
(4)   book a table for a dozen at your local Greek restaurant
      timed for 10.30 p.m. and drag your stragglers down
      there. It won't matter if there are one or two more or
      less than a dozen, but at least you'll get everyone out
      and finish reasonably early.
(5)   December is peak time for 'drinks', so hold one
      in the fourth week of January instead.

BRUNCH

At any time of year, brunch (a breakfast party held on
Sunday) is one of the most civilized occasions there is.
It's surprising that more of them aren't given. There are
two main types, the buffet and the sit-down, and the
dividing line is the number of people. With more than a
dozen or so, the sit-down breakfast becomes impossible
and you must resort to a buffet.

In summer, try to serve the meal out of doors, weather
permitting. In winter, light a fire in the sitting-room.

What food you offer is up to you. The most difficult
meal to serve is the traditional fry-up. Too many bits and
pieces are needed, all of which have to be got ready
at exactly the right time. Some dishes, such as braised
kidneys and sausages, will hold quite well; eggs have to
be done at the last minute; hash browns, fried potatoes
and fried bread are all bad keepers. Timing is everything,
but the party will be more fun if the guests help with the
cooking, while knocking back the buck's fizz.

An alternative is to serve kedgeree (see recipe on page 84), a delicious mixture of smoked fish, rice, onion and hard-boiled eggs. It won't hold for ever, but the rice and the onions will and you can quickly re-heat the fish and the eggs at the last minute and fold the dish together. An essential accompaniment to kedgeree is tomato ketchup; the combination is excellent. A more decadent, and surprisingly good combination, is kedgeree served with very thin slices of crisply grilled smoked streaky bacon.

Another idea, for summer, is to get a whole cooked ham, on the bone, and leave it out on the table for guests to carve their own slices. Boiled eggs and warm fresh rolls complete the ham-and-eggs breakfast.

Breakfast is also a good time for a barbecue, which means plenty of sausages, kidney, bacon and mushroom kebabs, grilled tomatoes and so on.

Another, very simple, possibility, especially if you plan to start much before noon, is to offer a basketful of baguettes and croissants, good-quality jam, unsalted butter and *café au lait*.

Whatever the food you serve for breakfast, you will be serving buck's fizz to drink. This splendid drink – 50-50 cheap dry sparkling wine and orange juice – will postpone and alleviate hangovers (although for severe cases a bloody mary may be necessary). The alternative morning drink, black velvet, is neither so popular nor so effective. Ask your friends to bring a bottle of sparkling wine, to ease the strain on your purse.

PARTY ADMINISTRATION

If the party is a house party, given by everyone together, the usual rule is to decide roughly how many people you want to have in total and divide the number equally amongst the hosts. The only disadvantage of this is that the guests may form themselves into cliques, so you end up having five small parties going on in one room at the same time. An alternative is to create a house guest list before you send out the invitations. Everyone starts off by suggesting a list of names, and the house as a whole invites all the guests. If there's a dispute about a particular guest, it is decided by a majority vote, so that someone who is generally disliked can be excluded.

The costs of the party are divided equally. A separate account named 'Party' is opened in the ledger and any expenditure by the house is recorded through the docket system.

If a party is specifically for one person in the house – for example, a big birthday party – then that person will usually pay for the party and invite most of the guests. In return for helping with the party, the others in the house will probably want to invite one or two special friends.

Dinner parties can be administered in one of two ways. If the party is quite expensive and the food is both more expensive and more elaborate than your normal meals, the cost of the meal should come out of the host's own finances, and he or she and everyone else will be signed out for the evening. If, on the other hand, it's not really a dinner party as such but just a matter of having friends round for supper and the food is the same sort of food as you'd be eating for a house meal anyway, then everyone who will be at the meal signs in on the meals chart and the host signs, for example, 'I+3' if he or she is having three guests. Everything he or she spends on the meal goes through the docket system.

CHAPTER 10

Affairs of the body and the heart

A shared house consisting of young single people of mixed sex is bound to create conditions for gossip and innuendo. Rules, ultimately, will be broken. When I first started living in shared houses, it seemed important to me that one kept love affairs separate from the simple business of sharing a house. I still think that principle is a sound one, but it doesn't always work out.

I once shared a house with a friend and a female colleague of his moved in. It took some months, but eventually the mutual attraction took hold and she and I ended up in bed together, and shortly afterwards we were asked by my friend to move out. This was because he and she did not get on too well; I was faced with the choice of staying with my friend or moving out with my lover. As it happened, a double room was available in the houseshare she had just left, so we joined that as a couple. I am afraid that our relationship deteriorated from then on, to the extent that we were hardly good company for the others in the house. The others in the house were also involved in a continuing saga of broken and remade affairs which lasted for the best part of three years until everyone finally seemed to settle into stable partnerships. Those partnerships, despite the fact that we all know what went on in those three years, are stable and enduring, and remarkably we are all still close friends. There are strains, of course, when those who were involved in particularly emotional affairs meet; somehow, despite our overall closeness, this does not happen often.

It's very easy, when one is single and in close companionship with someone of the opposite sex (I am assuming heterosexuality, since I can speak from experience and therefore understand the heterosexual mores; however, much of what I am saying may be equally applicable to relationships between gay men and women), to fall in love, and into bed. The problem with relationships of this sort is that the reason you are together is not primary attraction but another reason altogether – you just happen to live in the same house. This is not always the best ground on which to build a relationship. On the other hand, you will be familiar with your partners' idiosyncrasies outside the bedroom, you will have seen him or her pattering about in the early morning, you will know him or her warts and all, whereas the pick-up from a party can often provide a shock in the cold grey dawn of the morning after. The principal drawback to internal affairs is not that they are necessarily more fragile than external affairs: it is simply that when they break up the situation will be painful and difficult not just for the couple but for the whole household. It is easy to think that you know your new partner, having lived with him or her, but once the relationship has the added degree of intimacy that comes from being in love you both find out much more. In an 'external' affair you would be learning all this much more slowly over the course of many dates, dirty weekends and nights spent together. As soon as incompatibility looms, you can pull out of an external affair, but an internal affair is different. From the moment the first kiss is reciprocated, both of you are committed and pulling out will be painful. The risk is much, much greater with an internal affair, and my advice is not to get involved in one. Unfortunately, we humans don't have much control over our emotions and however much one knows it's a bad idea, one can easily get carried away in a tide of emotion and lust.

External affairs are, however, a different matter. A relaxed shared house is a much better environment than the family home for the consummation of an external affair since, with luck, your flatmates will hold sufficiently liberal views not to mind about your promiscuity. Most flatmates, however, are naturally curious about other people's sex lives and this can be a bit of a drawback. Indeed, a single flat is probably slightly better suited to the conduct of an affair. (The shared house comes into its own when the affair ends.) If you are conducting an external affair, you must be prepared to introduce your lover to your flatmates fairly soon. A one-night stand need not, of course, be introduced to all and sundry on the morning after, incongruously dressed in crumpled glad-rags and missing its toothbrush. But if your date comes to pick you up, it's a simple matter – besides being a common courtesy – to introduce him or her to all those who are in at the time. Later, of course, you can invite the new lover for a meal when everyone is in, and thus satisfy their understandable curiosity.

There are of course several stages to an affair, at one of which affairs very often stagnate. The first stage is just a matter of fancying; the second stage is what the Americans are pleased to call dating and what some mothers would call 'walking out'. Nowadays the physical consummation of the affair usually takes place during this stage; or it might be delayed until you are 'going steady'. Many affairs merely blunder on in the 'going steady' stage, dwindling from an excitement to a habit. The fourth stage is co-habitation, with or without marriage, and the fifth is procreation. Introducing your lover to your co-domesticates is something that should be done fairly early on during the second stage of your affair. By the time you are 'going steady' your lover will be almost part of the furniture and your co-domesticates will treat him or her as one of the 'family'.

The real difficulty in flatshares comes in the fourth and fifth stages. One of the flatsharing myths is that couples don't make good flatmates. As with most myths, there lies within it a tiny element of truth. Flatshares work if everyone wants to make them work; that means showing and feeling some kind of loyalty to one's other flatmates. But in the early months of an affair your lover may well worry about your loyalty to him or her, if you live in a mixed share. What may seem like averagely friendly behaviour on your part towards your other flatmates could be interpreted by your lover as outrageous promiscuity and infidelity. Before long you may find yourself in a hornet's nest of competing jealousies. If you or your lover should be given to jealousy at all, you would be doing everyone a favour if you fought your own little battles in the privacy of a poky little bedsit or studio flat.

On the other hand, if jealousy *isn't* a problem living as a couple in a flatshare can make co-habitation a lot less claustrophobic. You will have to be less intimate as a couple in the company of your flatmates, and be prepared to give up some of yourself and some of your partner to the flat. This type of arrangement can keep your relationship on a more free-and-easy level. You can go out for a night with your old mates, or work late at the office, confident that your other flatmates will keep your lover happy – and on the nights when he or she is out with his or her mates you don't have to sit at home moping but can still enjoy the company of others.

Living with a couple can be very awkward. To begin with, there's the 'intrusion' dilemma, which occurs when you come into the sitting room, say, and find the couple having a quick kiss and a cuddle: it's easy to think that you've just spoilt a bout of serious heavy petting and a highly intimate moment. Don't worry about it – the sitting room is yours just as much as it's theirs, and if they didn't want to be interrupted they should have gone upstairs to their own room. Whatever you do, don't blush till your dandruff turns pink and mumble apologetically before leaving the room. This will only make you look foolish. Instead, be bold, march in and offer to make everyone some tea. So what if they were kissing? Of course, if they were doing something a bit ruder than just kissing, you might be excused a little blush. But there's still no need to apologize. Just say 'Hi' and scarper, giving them time to re-adjust their clothing and persuade themselves that your entry was just a figment of their lurid imaginations.

This sort of situation can be a bit tricky if you are

lodging in a flat belonging to a young couple, because one of the enduring fantasies of many romantically inclined people is to make passionate love on a sheepskin rug in front of a roaring fire, and you may well be delaying the fulfilment of this fantasy by interrupting just as it was getting interesting. Don't worry about this. Like most fantasies, the sheepskin rug/open fire one is usually a huge disappointment in reality, particularly when the rug in question is sheepskin-look polyester and the fire in question is a coal-effect two-bar electric model incorporating a blown 'fire-glo' bulb. You're doing everyone a favour by keeping it in the realms of the imagination.

The next potential problem is that of partisanship. Don't get involved or take sides. Your flatmates' resident lovers are strictly off-limits. There's a code of honourable behaviour to which you should stick, and breaking up couples with whom you live is beyond the pale. If they're already on the verge of splitting, you as a flatmate are likely to get caught in the cross-fire. The best course of action is for women to take the woman's side and for men to take the man's side. That way you are less likely to get dragged in as co-respondent. Unfortunately, it's also possible to get dragged in on the other side, and this is where things get really whacky, particularly if there has been a bit of fancying beforehand. Yes, before you can say Cesare you have duplicated the Borgia household in your own flat. Would that it were possible to keep to honourable codes in such circumstances. More often than not affairs which started on the rebound end in tears and worse, but human emotions have little truck with reason or honour.

Impossible pashes
Impossible and unreturned pashes can make life very difficult in a shared house. Young or youngish women who develop a totally impractical pash for an older member of the household can be quite impossible, making the life of that older person hard to bear. Unfortunately, in this case as always, the pash does not respond to reason; but it might respond more effectively to a bit of gentle teasing. Exercise great care! Adolescents afflicted by pashes can

be unpredictable.

The converse of the impossible adolescent pash is the Obscure Object of Desire: a much younger woman in a predominantly male household after whose body the male residents lust. Provided that the men behave relatively honourably – and by and large they do – such a young woman has nothing to fear from them. The most effective restraint of their baser instincts is the presence of a female peer. In the meantime, the men can continue to dream, the obscure object of desire can pursue romance with the trendy young guys she knows outside the house or flat and she will be treated with the greatest possible courtesy by her flatmates, whom she will think are sweet and avuncular. Humph.

Real danger arises when an obscure object of desire develops an adolescent pash on one of her desirers. There are several possible outcomes:

(1) if the man's a cad and a bounder, he accidentally buys a six-pack of Crucial Brew on the night when he knows only the two of them will be at home, phones for a pizza and takes her to bed. They fornicate frequently for a fortnight. She thinks she's found true love, while he thinks he's found heaven for a fortnight. She gets herpes, he gets bored, she goes back to reading *My Guy*.

(2) if the man's a cad, he has a drink, comes home, finds her up, they couple, he feels guilty about it the next day and decides not to speak to her again – which is awkward for two people living in the same house. She gets wise, and wonders why it's taken so long to find out the truth about men.

(3) if the man's a gentleman he either (a) woos her but doesn't take her to bed until he's sure he loves her. Soon they get married and have lots of lovely babies and they all live happily ever after. (This outcome is rare.) Or (b) he smiles at her occasionally, dreams about her lithe young body nightly for a fortnight and then starts to pursue a much more suitable partner of his own age: she is madly but unreasonably jealous for a week.

Notes on etiquette

(1) It is not done to take early-morning tea or buck's fizz to your flatmate solely for the purpose of finding out whether she or he has 'pulled'.

(2) It is not done to take tea or fizz to your flatmate even if you know he or she has pulled *and* you take two cups or glasses (even worse, three).

(3) You may take early-morning tea or fizz for two if you know both partners well and are not just being nosey.

(4) It is not done to make impertinent remarks about strange toothbrushes in the bathroom.

(5) You should lend your new lover your dressing-gown. This way everyone else who bumps into him/her in the morning will know to whom he/she belongs.

(6) Do not use all the hot water for post-coital ablutions.

(7) Do try to introduce your lover to everyone who happens to be around. If you can't remember his or her name, invent one.

CHAPTER 11

Rows and how to enjoy them

Most married people have rows. If married folk have them, after an intensive selection process, how much more likely is a row in a shared house or flat where membership is decided by a far shorter and more random process than society's courtship rituals. In theory, however, one major cause of marital strife should not cause domestic rows. If you are fighting with your co-domesticate because of jealousy, infidelity or inadequate sexual performance you are reading the wrong chapter. Domestic rows specifically exclude rows for these marital or pseudo-marital reasons. That's not to say that the green-eyed monster, in particular, is not responsible for a good many rows between co-domesticates. The trouble is, it's breaking all the rules of co-domesticity to mention this, because no one is supposed to know. On the other hand, if the row is already in the final stages of bare-knuckle-dusting the rules no longer apply.

Every shared house must expect its fair share of rows. Some are unavoidable, so the aim should be to make them as painless as possible. On the other hand, if rows *can* be prevented they should be.

There are two main types of row: the roaring and the smouldering. Rows are in this respect like fires – a smouldering row can suddenly erupt into a roaring one, and after a roaring row there is usually a period of smouldering while the embers cool. Not all smouldering rows develop into full roaring rows – they usually need a little fanning for this to occur. Left on their own, smouldering rows can carry on smouldering, or can peter out of their own accord.

HOW TO DEAL WITH ROWS

Roaring rows
When dealing with a roaring row, there is a very real danger that you will become involved. It is usually better to maintain a safe distance until the roaring row has burned itself out and reduced to smouldering embers before approaching and attempting to douse the embers. All you can do with a roaring row is keep yourself, your valuables and other people out of harm's way.

Roaring rows usually cause the most immediate damage, but a smouldering row left unattended can cause a great deal of trouble and long-term resentment.

Smouldering rows
Smouldering rows should be put out as quickly as possible. If you cannot put out the smouldering row, one method of dealing with it is to let it burn out quickly, by fanning it to a controlled roaring row. Otherwise you have to deal with the row by dealing with one or more of its three essential components.

Professional fire-fighters tell us that a fire needs fuel, oxygen and heat to keep it burning. Rows need tension, dislike and a reason. Just as petrol and air do not need much heat to start blazing, high tension and strong dislike can burst into a roaring row without much of a reason. And once a row has started, it generates its own reason until you put it out. The reason is the spark, but the row feeds off the antipathy and the tension.

Prevention is better than cure with rows as well as fires. The best form of prevention is to control the dislike and the tension.

Personal dislike is hard to deal with. It occurs between two people and is usually there all the time, underneath rather than at the surface. If I don't like someone, I usually know about it fairly early on. Sometimes it takes longer, and dislike can result from an unpleasant experience or even a row. The trouble is, once the dislike is there it can only be hidden – it seldom goes away. If two of your co-domesticates don't get on, you would be best advised to ask one or other or both of them to leave. Very often each of them will blame the other, and expect the other to leave; in any case, sooner or later one of them will move in with a lover instead or buy his/her own place.

The best way to avoid the problems of personal dislike is to make as sure as possible that you are all reasonably compatible in the first place: this means advertising vacancies and making sure that everyone in the place has the opportunity to choose and veto potential co-domesticates. If there is a strong degree of personal antipathy between you and someone else, you should consider moving, because there really isn't much that can be done about it.

Rows are bred by tension. Modern city life is very stressful, owing to our competitive work and study environments and the pressures of travelling on congested roads or public transport. We get home after a bad day at work worn out, wound up and ready to take it out on our co-domesticates. Controlling rows is often just a matter of keeping down tension. Tension is easier to get rid of than dislike; the easiest way to do so is with drugs. Unfortunately, the most effective drugs are strongly addictive, or illegal or both. Alcohol and nicotine both work quite well, but they too are addictive. Having a gin and a cigarette as soon as you get in from work may make you feel human for five minutes but then you will need a stronger gin after the really bad day and before long you're cirrhotic. Nicotine is just plain disgusting, and if your co-domesticates don't smoke you're not going to help matters by lighting up. There really is only one substance which effectively reduces tension and is neither illegal nor particularly bad for you and that is tea. A cup of tea, made straight after you get in from work, works wonders; nothing else tastes quite as soothing and has so marked an effect on the nervous system. If you have tea most nights, you can keep the alcohol for the occasions when a more drastic remedy is called for. Furthermore, making a pot of tea is a simple and effective way of distributing goodwill amongst your flatmates. The tea-pot is an enduring symbol of cosy home life, and with very good reason.

Talking, too, often helps reduce tension caused by factors outside the house. You may remember talking into the small hours during your adolescence, consoling the poor person who was convinced that he/she was the only virgin left in school (that's funny, you always thought it was you), and you've probably decided that you have had enough of such heavy conversations. Besides, you now need your sleep and the idea of putting the world to rights until three in the morning just doesn't seem as important as it once did. But if you can unload some of your worries on to one of your co-domesticates' sympathetic shoulders, much of the general tension can be reduced – and you, too, should be prepared to return the favour.

Unfortunately, social mores prevent the use of another method of dealing with tension – giving each other a rub or a hug. We are all too hung up on the sexual aspect of touching, but if you can get relaxed enough with your co-domesticates to enjoy non-sexual touching you'll all be much the better for it. A very good way of easing tension is foot massage. Usually one has to be very drunk to consider foot massage, and hot feet that have been a long time inside woollen socks in leather shoes do tend to pong a bit. The biblical custom of foot-washing was intended to be relaxing and pleasurable, and having someone else wash and rub your feet is indeed enjoyable – if not nearly as kinky as it sounds. As an alternative to massage, a hot bath helps reduce tension and is all the more effective if it is preceded by forty minutes of vigorous exercise.

The third element of a row is the reason for starting it. If you've got lots of tension and dislike, you don't need much of a reason, but if you all like each other and are on the whole quite laid-back, you'll need a pretty good reason to start a row. Here are 50 good reasons for a row:

(1) Leave toenail clippings on the bathroom floor.
(2) Tell your friends to phone after 11 p.m. on weekdays.

(3) Use the last of the milk.

(4) Use the last of the loo roll.

(5) Use today's paper to light the fire.

(6) Scratch the Sade LPs.

(7) Rustle the *FT* all through *Dallas.*

(8) 'Borrow' his/her Walkman batteries.

(9) Play Meatloaf through the loudspeakers.

(10) Swap your Marillion tape for his/her Alison Moyet in his/her Walkman.

(11) Borrow his/her bike and leave the seat in the wrong position.

(12) Dismantle your bike in the sitting room, and lose a vital bit so it stays there indefinitely.

(13) Use the dressmaking scissors for carpet-laying.

(14) Leave the sitting-room door open, persistently.

(15) Slam the sitting-room door shut.

(16) Hog the bathroom at 8.15 in the morning.

(17) Use the last of someone else's shampoo or bubble-bath.

(18) Use any of someone else's expensive ditto.

(19) Leave leg or face shavings in the bath or basin.

(20) Take the bookmark out of *War and Peace.*

(21) Be cheerful before noon.

(22) Forget to pass on urgent phone messages.

(23) Leave the top off the toothpaste.

(24) Do anything whatsoever with chewing-gum.

(25) Save the dripping (yes, I know your mother does but *she* still thinks that fat is rationed).

(26) Don't wash up.

(27) Don't wash up your scrambled-egg saucepan.

(28) Leave your cereal bowl to harden.

(29) Leave the last of the milk out overnight in warm weather.

(30) Borrow some hair gel and don't put the lid on properly.

(31) Video the boxing over *Diva.*

(32) Watch American football.

(33) Unplug the video just before *Arsenic and Old Lace.*

(34) Be rude to the new lover.

(35) Talk about football.

(36) Ignore someone's new haircut.
(37) Leave Marmite in the butter.
(38) Leave peanut butter on the breadknife.
(39) Use a wet spoon for the sugar.
(40) Grill fish and just rinse the grill pan.
(41) Bring your mates in for *Trivial Pursuit* after the pub on Tuesday night.
(42) Leave your underwear to dry on the sitting-room radiator.
(43) Tell him/her that he/she needs to lose about 19 lbs.
(44) Talk with your mouth full.
(45) Masticate with your mouth open.
(46) Don't put records away in their sleeves.
(47) Hide the corkscrew.
(48) Get your mates even more drunk on his/her 25-year-old malt.
(49) Take his/her vintage port to a party.
(50) Use his/her eyeliners for a fancy-dress party.

Afterword

Most shared houses and flats are for the young: shared living covers the period in a person's life between leaving home – with its secure nuclear foundations – and setting up a home of one's own. As people get married later and prolong their independence, so the need for shared living has arisen. I have benefited greatly from eight years (to date) in shared houses; it is a style of living which suits me.

I think it suits others, too. It encourages tolerance and understanding of other people and recognizes the fact that the human animal is a gregarious animal which thrives on intimate relationships – not necessarily sexual – as well as on more superficial social contacts. However, the trends are against me. While the population of Great Britain remains steady or falling, the rate of household formation is rising. More and more people are living lonely lives in single flats, often little more than shoe-boxes. Many of these are young people, anxious to get on the property ladder by buying the smallest place they can afford. I do not believe that this trend is good for society, but it is encouraged by the tax and financial laws, particularly the recent removal of multiple tax relief from homes in shared ownership.

Despite the lack of tax relief, shared living still has its advantages. Moreover, many of the new single households are comprised of older people whose children have left home. Is shared living an answer to some of the problems of an ageing population? Should there be more

Golden Girls – or Golden Boys – among us? I think that this could be an answer to a growing problem. Although older people cherish independence as much as anyone, as age advances the body deteriorates and the proximity of others who can offer company, and, in an emergency, alert the health professionals before it is too late, is a valuable safety net.

Much of the advice in this book is as valid for the old as it is for the young, and all of it, whether you decide to accept or reject it, is born of experience. I hope some of it may make your life as a flat- or housesharer a little easier to cope with – and maybe even more rewarding than I have found mine.

APPENDIX

Sample flatsharing agreements

There are two agreements here: the first might be used when the landlord is resident, and the second for a non-resident landlord. They are both written in the form of words which will indicate that there is a licence rather than a tenancy. If you, as a tenant, are fortunate enough to be offered an agreement which clearly describes you as 'tenant' and the landlord as 'landlord' in those words, then you will be in a strong position. However, most shared houses are let on individual licence, since this generally gives the landlord a better chance of being able to obtain possession in the event of a dispute.

Housing law is not static; it changes almost by the day. Under the present government (1989) it is moving back towards favouring landlords rather than tenants; this may result in more rented accommodation coming on to the market, but almost certainly at higher rents.

The net result is that these agreements are only a **guide**. If you are in doubt about your rights, don't hesitate to seek advice – either from a solicitor, a Citizen's Advice Bureau or a local Law Centre. This applies particularly in Scotland and Northern Ireland, where the legal system is different from that in England and Wales. Most of the difference lies in the legal terminology used: your rights as a citizen are by and large the same (although there are some glaring exceptions – for example in the laws on homosexual acts, and the liquor licensing laws).

Always read any agreement you are offered very carefully, and if you don't like a term of the agreement then ask the landlord if he or she would mind it being changed or deleted. Very often landlords say that in fact they don't mind overnight guests but they still insist on the term prohibiting them in the agreements. If you can, make sure that you have another person present when you talk to the landlord – but of course, you, the tenant, are always in a weak bargaining position.

The agreements aim to create, in both cases, *contractual licences*. However, as explained in Chapter 5, whether or not there is a licence, a tenancy or a restricted contract depends upon the *facts* in each case, rather than the wording of any agreement. For there to be a licence, which puts the lodger outside the protection of the Rent Acts, there must have been no intention to grant exclusive possession of the whole or of any part of the property. For example, if the landlord were to issue each lodger with a key to his or her personal room – as sometimes happens in blocks or bedsits – there is *prima facie* evidence that the lodger has exclusive possession of the room and therefore a tenancy rather than a licence to occupy: this would give much greater protection under the Rent Acts. Note that this makes little difference if the landlord is resident, because with a resident landlord you have very little security in any case.

Both agreements have two clauses which are normal but irritating. The first of these prohibits animals on the premises without separate permission. Animals can damage furniture, they deposit hair and can bring in fleas – and resident landlords may have their own pets who tend not to be so hospitable to visitors as their owners. If the place is grotty, a non-resident landlord may not object to your keeping a cat – but if you do so without asking him or her first it might place whatever security of tenure you may have at risk. The second clause is a restriction on guests. In the first agreement, the proviso is that you ask the landlord's permission – which, since you share homes, is the normal courtesy in any case and should not usually be refused. In the second agreement, the proviso is that you only have guests for two nights in any seven – which would allow for your friend to come down for the weekend, and for someone to stay over after the buses have stopped. If you've been given an agreement that has a total ban on overnight guests, then try asking for that term to be changed. The clause is intended to prevent a lodger from taking a permanent partner or an additional lodger, whose presence would place an additional burden on the shared facilities of the property which might cause inconvenience to others.

AGREEMENT WHERE LANDLORD IS RESIDENT

This agreement is worded fairly simply, but covers most of the potential problems. The basis of a relationship with a resident landlord is close and personal, but the agreement forms the legal backbone to the relationship.

LICENCE AGREEMENT
between

....

(hereinafter referred to as the Owner)
and

....

(hereinafter referred to as the Occupier)
in respect of

....

(hereinafter referred to as the Premises)
for a consideration of
£. . . . . per calendar month paid monthly in advance

WHEREAS

1.   The Owner has the right to possession of the Premises but is willing for the time being to share them

2.   The Occupier wishes to take occupation as a contractual licensee on the terms set out which are understood

3.   The Occupier accepts that the Owner may wish at any time to obtain possession of the whole of the premises on short notice

4. The Occupier has no right of exclusive occupation in the Premises or in any part of the Premises

and

5. The Owner may at any time require the exclusive occupation of the whole of the Premises as a home for himself or for his immediate family

IT IS AGREED THAT

1. The Owner shall allow the Occupier to have non-exclusive occupation of the Premises which the Occupier shall share with the Owner, members of the Owner's immediate family and any other persons whom the Owner may permit to occupy the Premises.

2. The Occupier shall:
(a) pay the consideration on the days and in the amounts aforesaid without making any deductions
(b) not make any alteration in, or addition to the Premises, nor attach anything to the walls without the permission of the Owner
(c) not do, nor allow others to do on the Premises anything which might become a nuisance to or annoy the other occupiers or the neighbours
(d) preserve the furniture and effects of which he has the main use from being destroyed or damaged. An inventory of the furniture and fittings of which the Occupier has the main use is set out in the Schedule annexed hereto
(e) preserve all other furniture and effects on the Premises from being damaged or destroyed as a result of his actions or those of his guests
(f) not remove any furniture or effects from the Premises, nor from room to room, nor bring in any item of his own, without the consent of the Owner
(g) not carry on any trade or business on the Premises
(h) make a fair contribution towards the cleaning of the Premises
(i) keep any areas of which he has the main use reasonably clean

(j) pay to the Owner an agreed share of the cost of all gas and electricity supplied to the Premises during the occupancy including fixed and standing charges

(k) pay to the Owner a fair portion of the cost of the telephone service, including line and equipment rental and call charges, as the Owner shall at his absolute discretion determine

(l) not bring on the Premises any oil heater or flammable or dangerous substance

(m) not allow rubbish to accumulate on the premises

(n) not allow visitors on to the Premises except with the permission of the Owner

(o) not play any musical instrument or television, radio or gramophone or similar equipment in a manner which might disturb the other occupiers or the neighbours between the hours of midnight and 7 a.m.

(p) not keep any animal on the Premises without the consent of the Owner

3.   The Premises shall only be occupied by the Owner, members of his immediate family, the Occupier and no more than . . . . . other occupiers.

4.   This Agreement can be terminated by either side giving 28 days' notice unless any of the terms are broken, when the Owner can terminate the Agreement by giving two days' notice.

5.   The Owner has full control over the Premises at all times and reserves the right to enter any part of the Premises for cleaning, maintenance and any other reasonable purpose whatsoever including the possible discovery of breaches of this Agreement, and to authorize others to do so on his behalf

Signed and witnessed:
(Date) (Owner) (Occupier) (Witness)
N.B. in Scotland, two witnesses should sign

AGREEMENT WHERE LANDLORD IS NON-RESIDENT

This agreement is the sort of agreement a non-resident

landlord is likely to offer you in England and Wales; in Scotland and Northern Ireland it may be slightly but not signifi-
cantly different. It gives you some idea of the usual terms to a licence. If the landlord gives you no agreement to sign, do not suggest that he uses this one, but *do* insist on receipts for any rent you pay – and you will probably have a tenancy. If you plan to let a house you don't live in to sharers, ask a solicitor to draw up a licence agreement on similar terms to this one.

The agreement contains a clause which would allow the landlord to claim possession under one of the nine mandatory grounds for granting possession in the Rent Acts if the landlord wishes to use the property as home for himself or his immediate family, should the courts eventually decide that, despite the words, there was a tenancy. It is, if you like, a fail-safe clause. It won't work, however, unless the landlord really does want it as home for himself or his immediate family; he can't use it to get you out just because he doesn't like the look of your face.

LICENCE AGREEMENT

between

....
(hereinafter referred to as the Owner)
and

....
(hereinafter referred to as the Occupier)
in respect of

....
(hereinafter referred to as the Premises)
for a consideration of
£ . . . . . per calendar month paid monthly in advance

WHEREAS

1.   The Owner wishes to obtain vacant possession of very short notice and the Occupier accepts the fundamental term and condition of the Agreement that no tenancy is created but there is a mere right to occupy the Premises as a contractual licensee

2.   The Occupier wishes to take occupation on the terms set out which are understood and accepted

3.   This Agreement is not extended to provide security of tenure as set out in the Rent Acts 1977 or any similar enactment

4.   There is no right of exclusive occupation in the Premises or any part thereof

5.   The Owner may at any time in the future wish to occupy the Premises as a home for himself or for his immediate family

NOW IT IS AGREED THAT

1.   The Owner shall permit the Occupier to have non-exclusive occupation of the Premises and reserves the right to place other persons in the Premises

2.   The Occupier shall:
(a)   pay the consideration on the days and in the manner aforesaid clear of all deductions
(b)   not make any alterations or additions to the Premises nor attach anything to the walls without the written permission of the Owner or his authorized agent
(c)   not do or allow any other person to do on the Premises anything which may become a nuisance or annoyance to the Owner, any other occupiers or the occupiers of adjoining or neighbouring premises or commit any illegal or immoral acts
(d)   preserve the furniture and effects from being destroyed or damaged and keep all electrical and mechanical equipment in good working order. An inventory of such furniture and fittings and their condition is set out in the Schedule annexed hereto
(e)   not remove any of the furniture and effects from

the Premises or move the items from one room to another or move in any item of furniture of his own without the written consent of the Owner or his authorized agent

(f) not create any sub-occupancy or any like right in the premises nor allow any children to share or use the Premises without the written consent of the Owner or his authorized agent

(g) not carry on any profession or trade or business on the Premises

(h) leave the Premises at the expiration of the occupancy in the same clean state and condition as they were at the beginning of the occupancy and make good or pay for the repair or replacement of all such articles as shall be broken, lost, damaged or destroyed during the occupancy

(j) at the expiration of the occupancy pay for any cleaning of the Premises and for any cleaning of fabrics and furniture on the Premises as the Owner or his authorized agent may deem to be necessary

(k) jointly and severally with the other occupiers (if any) of the Premises pay for all gas and electricity supplied to the Premises during the occupancy including fixed and standing charges

(l) jointly and severally with the other occupiers (if any) of the Premises pay all the charges incurred for the use of the telephone including rental of lines and equipment and any fixed or standing charges

(m) not bring on to the Premises any oil heater or other appliance or any flammable or dangerous substance which might endanger the fabric of the Premises and its occupants or affect the Owner's insurance cover

(n) not allow any rubbish to accumulate on the Premises

(p) not allow visitors to remain on the Premises between the hours of 2 a.m. and 7 a.m. except as overnight guests, and not to allow any overnight guests on the Premises for more than two nights in any seven

(q) not play any musical instrument or television or radio or gramophone or similar equipment between the hours of midnight and 7 a.m. except in such a manner as shall be inaudible to the other occupiers of the Premises (if any) and to the neighbours

(r)   not keep any animal on the Premises without the written consent of the Owner or his authorized agent

3.   The Premises shall not be occupied by any person or persons other than the Occupier or other person or persons selected by the Owner as hereinafter set out. The Owner reserves the right to place other occupiers in the Premises up to a maximum of ..... occupiers and the Occupier shall raise no objection thereto, but without prejudice to the Owner's absolute right under Clause 1 of this Agreement the Owner shall consult with the Occupier before making the final selection of an additional Occupier

4.   This Agreement shall be terminable on 28 days' notice being given by either party but if any of the terms of this Agreement are broken the Owner may terminate the Agreement on two days' notice without prejudice to any rights of the Owner to claim sums owing as compensation or damage

5.   The Owner has full control over the Premises at all times and reserves the right having given not less than 24 hours' notice to enter the Premises at all reasonable times to undertake maintenance and other services and for any other reasonable purpose whatsoever including the possible discovery of any breaches of the terms of this Agreement, and to authorize his agent or servants to do so on his behalf

In witness whereof we have this day set our hands,
(Date) (Owner) (Occupier) (Witness)
N.B. in Scotland, there should be two witnesses

Index

shift work 62
shirts, washing and
  ironing 101-4
shopping 63
single sex shares 4
sitting room 86;
  cleaning 90
Sony walkman 88
stereos 88
students 1
student slum 6
Student Union Notice
  Board 16
sub-tenants 29
suits 105;
  polyester 22
Sunday supper
  noodles 82
sweet peppers 70

takeaway cartons 90
tax and mortgages 50
tea 63, 65;
  to avoid rows 130

teddy-bear method 25
telephone 32
the interview 20
thrashes 109
ties 106
Times, The 16
timewarp 11
tomatoes 70
trolleys, shopping,
  noisy 63
TV 87
type of sharer (in
  ad) 17

vegetables 68
vegetable stew 80
video recorder 87
virility 4
vomit 6

washing machines 98
washing up 107
water rates 31
windowsill, kitchen 9